The Future
of Europe

Uniting Vision, Values and Citizens?

Jesuit Centre for Faith and Justice

First published 2006 by
Veritas Publications
7/8 Lower Abbey Street
Dublin 1
Ireland
Email publications@veritas.ie
Website www.veritas.ie

10 9 8 7 6 5 4 3 2 1

10-ISBN 1-85390-992-0
13-ISBN 978-1-85390-992-4

Copyright © Jesuit Centre for Faith and Justice, 2006

A catalogue record for this book is available from the British Library.

Designed and typeset by Paula Ryan
Printed in the Republic of Ireland by Betaprint, Dublin

Veritas books are printed on paper made from the wood pulp of managed forests. For every tree felled, at least one tree is planted, thereby renewing natural resources.

Contents

Contributors

Bertie Ahern TD is Taoiseach of Ireland. He was first elected to Dáil Éireann in 1977 and has represented Dublin Central since 1981. He has been Taoiseach since June 1997. He served as Assistant Government Whip (1980–1981); Minister of State at the Department of the Taoiseach and the Department of Defence, and Government Chief Whip (1982); Minister for Labour (1987–1991); Minister for Industry and Commerce (1993); Minster for Finance (1991–1994); Minister for Arts, Culture and the Gaeltacht (1994) and Tánaiste (1994). He has been leader of Fianna Fáil since 1994 and served as Lord Mayor of Dublin in 1986–1987.

David Begg is Secretary General of the Irish Congress of Trade Unions. Prior to his appointment to that post in 2001, he was Chief Executive of Concern Worldwide. He is a Director of the Central Bank, a Governor of The Irish Times Trust, a member of the National Economic and Social Council, and of the Advisory Board for Irish Aid. He is also a member of the Executive Committee of the European Trade Union Confederation. He was the chairperson of the Democracy Commission, established in 2003, whose final report, *Engaging Citizens: The Case for Democratic Renewal in Ireland*, was published in October 2005.

Peter Bosch is an official of the European Commission and is heading a team responsible for developing external policies on migration and asylum in the Immigration and Asylum Unit of the Directorate-General Justice, Freedom and Security. He is involved in preparing policy papers of the European Commission and was an advisor to the Global Commission on International Migration which presented its final report to the UN Secretary General in October 2005. He is a graduate of Erasmus University, Rotterdam.

Jean-Pierre Bou is an official of the European Commission, where he works on the external aspects on migration policy in the Immigration and Asylum Unit of Directorate-General Justice, Freedom and Security. He deals primarily with relations with African, Mediterranean and Latin American countries and with the linkages between migration and development. He is a graduate of the Institut d'Etudes Politiques, Paris and of the College of Europe, Bruges.

Noel Coghlan served in a variety of positions in the European Commission, including that of Chef de Cabinet Adjoint to the Irish Member of the Commission from 1976 to 1981. Prior to his EU appointments, he worked in the Department of Finance in Dublin and with the World Bank. Since his retirement in 1999, he has campaigned for debt relief and is currently a Director of the Debt and Development Coalition. He is a graduate of The London School of Economics and Political Science.

Alan Dukes is Director General of the Institute of European Affairs. Fine Gael Party leader from 1987 to 1990, he was a member of Dáil Éireann from 1981 to 2002 and at various times during that period was Minister for Agriculture; Minister for Finance; Minister for Justice; Minister for Transport, Energy and Communications. He has also been a Governor of the IMF and of the World Bank. He is currently a public affairs consultant and has worked extensively on EU technical assistance programmes with central and eastern European nations. He is also Chairman of the Alliance Française in Dublin.

John Gormley TD is a Green Party member of Dáil Éireann, representing Dublin South East. First elected to the Dáil in 1997, he is the Green Party's spokesperson on Foreign Affairs, Defence, and Health and Children and was elected as its first Cathaoirleach in 2002. He was one of the six people chosen by the Taoiseach to represent Ireland in the Convention on the Future of Europe, which drew up the draft EU Constitutional Treaty. He was a member of the Defence Working Group of the Convention and drafted a submission on the 'citizen's initiative', an issue which was subsequently included in the Constitution. He is the author of *Green Guide for Ireland* (1990).

Emma Haddad is a policy advisor in the Immigration and Asylum Unit of Directorate-General Justice, Freedom and Security in the European Commission. She specialises in the external policy aspect of migration, focusing on relations with countries outside the European Union. The holder of a PhD in international relations from the European Institute of The London School of Economics and Political Science, her thesis looked at the interplay between refugees and international society. Recent publications include contributions to *Global Society, The International Journal of Human Rights* and the *Encyclopaedia of International Relations and Global Politics*.

Robin Hanan is Coordinator of the European Anti Poverty Network (EAPN) Ireland, a membership network affiliated to the European Anti Poverty Network. He chairs the EAPN 'Review Group on Social Inclusion', is an alternate member of the European Economic and Social Committee and a part-time lecturer on 'Ireland in Europe' in UCD. From 1994 to 1999 he was Coordinator of Comhlámh, the association of development workers in global solidarity, and before that was a civil servant in several government departments.

Diarmuid Martin is Catholic Archbishop of Dublin. He was appointed Coadjutor Archbishop of Dublin in May 2003 and became Archbishop of Dublin in April 2004. He was ordained to the priesthood in 1969, following which he worked in the Archdiocese of Dublin, and then in 1976 was appointed to the secretariat of the Pontifical Council for the Family, in the Vatican. In 1986 he became Under-Secretary of the Pontifical Council for Justice and Peace, and in 1994 Secretary of the same Council. He was appointed Bishop in 1999 and Archbishop in 2001. In 2001, he was assigned as Permanent Observer of the Holy See at the United Nations Office and Specialised Agencies and at the World Trade Organisation in Geneva.

Nuria Molina is Policy and Development Officer with the European Anti Poverty Network (EAPN) in Brussels. She was Executive Officer with UBUNTU World Forum of Civil Society Networks from 2000 to 2005, following which she undertook a short-term post at the Financing for Development Office at the United Nations in New York. She studied Political Science at the University of Barcelona, The London School of Economics and Political Science, and the College of Europe, Bruges.

Dan O'Brien is a senior editor at the Economist Intelligence Unit, the business information arm of The Economist Group, whose functions include providing economic and political forecasts for over 200 countries. London-based, he specialises in political and economic affairs in Europe and global trade and investment issues. His role involves contributions to the broadcast media and to publications such as the *International Herald Tribune*, *The Wall Street Journal Europe* and *The Economist*. He was previously employed in the foreign service of the European Commission and as a teacher of economics. He is a graduate of University College Dublin.

Annelise Oeschger is the Secretary for International Relations at the Brussels office of ATD Fourth World, the international anti-poverty movement. She is also the representative of ATD at the Council of Europe. Since 2004 she has been President of the Conference of Council of Europe International Non-Governmental Organisations and Chair of the International NGO Liaison Committee. A Swiss national, she trained as a lawyer. She has been a member of the Voluntariat of ATD Fourth World since 1983, with assignments in Switzerland, France and Germany.

Gerry O'Hanlon SJ is a theologian and a staff member of the Jesuit Centre for Faith and Justice. He is also Associate Professor at the Milltown Institute. From 1998 to 2004 he was Provincial of the Irish Jesuit Province. He is author of *The Immutability of God in the Theology of Hans Urs von Balthasar* (1990) and of many articles on theology published in a range of journals, including *Irish Theological Quarterly*, *Milltown Studies*, *The Way*, *Doctrine and Life* and *The Furrow*.

John Palmer is a member of the Governing Board and former Political Director of the European Policy Centre, Brussels. He is also Deputy Chairman of the Centre's Political Europe programme. While Political Director he was Editor-in-Chief of the Centre's on-line public policy journal, *Challenging Europe*. He is an experienced radio and television broadcaster in both English and French, and between 1975 and 1997 was the Brussels-based European editor of *The Guardian*. He is the author of three books on European affairs: *Europe Without America: The Crisis in Atlantic Relations* (1987); *Trading Places: The Future of the European Community* (1989); *1992 and Beyond: The European Community into the 21ˢᵗ Century* (1991).

Doris Peschke is Secretary of the Churches' Commission for Migrants in Europe, an ecumenical agency of churches in Europe which deals with migration, asylum and anti-racism issues. She held an internship with the World Council of Churches' Programme to Combat Racism in 1981, worked for the representation of the Namibian liberation movement, SWAPO, in Berlin from 1983 to 1988, and as Secretary of the Churches' Development Services of the Protestant Church in Hesse and Nassau from 1988 to 1999. She was born in Hannover, Germany and holds qualifications in theology and ecumenical studies.

Peter Sutherland is Chairman of Goldman Sachs International and of BP plc. A graduate of civil law, he practiced at the Bar from 1969 to 1981. He has served as Attorney General of Ireland, EC Commissioner responsible for Competition Policy, Director General of GATT and subsequently of WTO. He is Chairman of the Trilateral Commission (Europe) and Foundation Board member of the World Economic Forum. He is Goodwill Ambassador for the United Nations Industrial Development Organization, and in January 2006 was appointed Special Representative for Migration by UN Secretary-General, Kofi Annan.

Olive Towey works with Concern Worldwide, an international humanitarian organisation working in thirty countries across the developing world. She joined the External Relations division of Concern in the run-up to Ireland's 2003 Presidency of the EU, and focuses on public and policy work in relation to European development issues. In 2005, she coordinated the Concern MakePovertyHistory campaign. She was previously coordinator of a coalition of sixteen organisations including NGOs, trade unions and state bodies whose work led to the establishment in 2006 of Connect Global Awareness and Media, which aims to raise awareness of development through partnership with the media.

Noel Treanor is Secretary General of the Commission of the Bishops' Conferences of the European Community, in Brussels. He has worked for COMECE since 1989 and has been Secretary General since 1993. He has published articles on various aspects of European policy, Church–State relationships in Europe, and the Churches and European integration in reviews published throughout Europe. He is a priest of the diocese of Clogher.

Gillian Wylie is a lecturer in International Peace Studies at the Irish School of Ecumenics, Trinity College Dublin. Her teaching and research interests are in the areas of international politics; civil society; politics and democratisation in eastern Europe; transnational social movements; the European Union; feminist and gender issues. She has published journal articles on a range of topics and is a member of the editorial board of *Studies, An Irish Quarterly Review*. She holds a PhD from the University of Aberdeen.

Acknowledgements

The Jesuit Centre for Faith and Justice would like to thank the contributors to this publication; it greatly appreciates the time and work they devoted to the preparation of their papers.

The Centre thanks also Fergus O'Donoghue SJ, editor of *Studies, An Irish Quarterly Review*, for permission to reprint papers by the following contributors: An Taoiseach, Bertie Ahern TD, David Begg, Noel Coghlan, Alan Dukes, Nuria Molina and Robin Hanan, Dan O'Brien, Doris Peschke and Peter Sutherland. These papers were originally published in *Studies*, Vol. 94, No. 375, autumn 2005.

Funding for the conference and public meetings at which several of the papers in this publication were originally presented was provided by the European Commission (Directorate General for Education and Culture), the Irish Province of the Society of Jesus and the Communicating Europe Initiative of the Department of Foreign Affairs. The Jesuit Centre for Faith and Justice is grateful to these bodies for their generous support.

Finally, the Centre thanks Máire Ní Chearbhaill for her assistance in editing the book, and the staff of Veritas, in particular Ruth Garvey, Paula Ryan and Caitriona Clarke, for their work in preparing the book for publication.

Foreword

The accession of ten new Members States on 1 May 2004 marked an historically significant expansion of the European Union: having started as a common market of six western European countries it now became a union of twenty-five, including seven former communist countries of central and eastern Europe.

The draft EU Constitutional Treaty, ageed at the June 2004 European Summit in Dublin, both symbolised deepening integration and provided the institutional structures for the more effective working of an enlarged Union. Just a year later, however, the process of ratifying the Treaty was spectacularly derailed by 'No' votes in referenda held in France and The Netherlands. The referendum results gave rise not only to uncertainty about the future of the proposed Constitution but to a recognition that public support for the process of European integration could not be taken for granted and that a gap had developed between the concerns of the citizens of Europe and the agenda of its leaders.

In June 2005, the EU Heads of State and Government agreed that there should be 'a pause for reflection' during which Member States and their peoples should engage in active debate about the future of Europe. With the aim of making a contribution to that debate, the Jesuit Centre for Faith and Justice, which undertakes social and theological analysis of issues of structural injustice, and *Studies, An Irish Quarterly Journal*, held a series of public events in Dublin in autumn 2005. These were a day-long conference, 'The Future of Europe – Uniting Vision, Values and Citizens?', held on 27 September 2005 and two public meetings: 'The Future of Europe – Challenges for Faith and Values', held on 26 September 2005, and 'Europe's Role in the World: Globalisation and Global Institutions', held on 24 October 2005.

The Future of Europe: Uniting Vision, Values and Citizens? includes papers presented at these events, as well as a number of articles commissioned specially for this publication. The aim is to explore the 'vision and values' that underpin the European Union, and how these find expression in political choices, institutional structures, economic policies and social priorities. The themes considered may be clustered into six broad groups.

Firstly, the question of balancing the development of 'an ever closer Union' with the preservation of national identity is explored. The task of fostering a 'European identity' in a Union that has Member States, twenty official languages and includes around 457 million people poses a major challenge. Furthermore, this process needs to respect the powerful appeal of national identity and allegiances. The further expansion of the European Union, including the possibility of Turkish membership, adds to the complexity of these issues.

The second theme concerns the active engagement of citizens in the decision-making processes of the European Union. Democracy is one of the fundamental principles of the European project, yet a 'democratic deficit' within its institutions and processes has come to be regarded as one of its major failings. The perception of the EU as a top-down project driven by 'elites' and having little or no relevance to or input from its citizens has dangerous potential. Connecting with the concerns and needs of its citizens is a prerequisite if the European project is to be sustainable.

The third theme is the balance between economic and social progress. Increased economic globalisation has challenged Europe's economies and raised questions about the sustainability of its systems of social protection. These issues have been given particular focus by slow growth and high unemployment in some of the larger EU countries. Achieving the twin goals of optimising economic growth and employment and maintaining social protections presents Europe with some difficult choices. How it responds will have huge implications for the welfare of each person, but particularly for those who suffer economic and social deprivation.

A fourth theme is Europe's relationship with the wider world. This raises the issue of the desirability and feasibility of a common EU foreign and security policy. It raises also questions about the role that Europe might play as a model and advocate for the development of a democratic and effective system of global governance, and for the protection of human rights throughout the world. A particular urgency attaches to Europe's response to global inequality, tragically evident in the impoverishment of millions of people in Europe's neighbouring continent, Africa. Here the challenge relates not just to aid and development policies of the EU and its Member States but to their willingness to adopt fair policies in international trade.

A fifth and related theme is Europe's response to migration and asylum in the context of the significant increase world wide in the movement of peoples over the last half-century. Heightened security concerns following 9/11, the financial costs of administering asylum and immigration systems, and the cultural challenges of absorbing large numbers of foreign nationals ensure that migration is one of the most controversial dynamics occurring in Europe. The EU has articulated its policy in terms of 'An Area of Justice, Freedom and Security'. But what does this policy mean in reality for migrants and host communities? What type of Europe is emerging – 'Fortress Europe' or 'Opportunity Europe'?

A sixth theme is the contribution which Christian values and beliefs might make to the process of bringing the peoples of European nations together. Christianity has been one of the most powerful forces shaping Europe, but in an increasingly secular and consumerist context the impact of its message on people's lives and on political events has diminished significantly. Yet Christianity's vision of the deeper possibilities of what it means to be human, and the emphasis in Church social teaching on values such as solidarity, subsidiarity and the common good, represent rich resources that can inspire and sustain the process of creating a unified and just Europe.

When the European project was started, its objectives were clear – a peaceful Europe built on core principles of human rights, democracy, social and economic solidarity. As the circumstances which gave urgency to the original project have passed into history, the hope and idealism that motivated its foundation seem to have diminished. There is a danger that they will be replaced by indifference, and even cynicism and suspicion. Redefining its mission and rebuilding solidarity are key challenges for the future of Europe. The choices now being made by European citizens and institutions will determine whether the Europe of the future is relegated to being 'just Europe' or will aspire to be 'a just Europe'.

Eugene Quinn
Director
Jesuit Centre for Faith and Justice
June 2006

Where Does the European Union Go Now?[1]

Bertie Ahern TD

The phrase, 'The Future of Europe – Uniting Visions, Values and Citizens?', succinctly summarises the nature of the challenge facing the European Union and its Member States. Of course, 'uniting vision, values and citizens' very accurately describes the development of Europe over the last half-century. Amidst all the current commentary about disillusionment with the European project, it is easy to forget the visionary nature of the European Union itself. Unlike practically every other political unit on the planet, the European Union was not forged through battle or conflict. It is not based around a single group regarding itself as a nation. It does not correlate with or correspond to any other form of federal or national government. And yet, it is not a purely multilateral organisation. The European Union is a unique political structure, which has been uniquely successful in the last half century.

The Union has been built around a core vision. That vision is of a political cooperation between independent Member States involving the pooling of sovereignty. That vision is based on respect. The European Union has never been based, and could never be based, on coercion. All of its members freely gave their consent to join.

If we are to identify the recipe for future success, I feel that we must carefully identify the elements that have led to the current success of the European Union. To my mind these elements can be summarised under four headings.

Firstly, the European Union has been based on democracy and the rule of law and is open only to states where these are a given. It is worth recalling that, were one to select one seventy-year old citizen from each of the Member States, only two – the Irish person and the Swede – would have lived in a country which has not known dictatorship, foreign aggression or invasion during his or her lifetime.

The European Union has been an essential contributor to the spreading of democracy in Europe. In doing so, it has also played a key role in eliminating the scope for warfare and conflict between the states of Europe. One only needs to look at the recent history of the western Balkans to see how fragile peace can be.

Secondly, the European Union has been based on economic cooperation amongst Member States, supplemented by assistance and solidarity between them. This economic cooperation has been a major engine of economic growth and prosperity. I am convinced it will continue to be so. Europe is more than a free trade area. We have built fair and transparent arrangements for the management of trade, for the regulation of industry, for the setting of minimum environmental and social standards and for the support of economic cohesion and agriculture. All of these have helped create the public confidence within Member States which makes European cooperation possible.

Thirdly, the Union has crafted a common approach to the rest of the world. This approach has been built very much on what one could call soft power – development aid, strong support for multilateral engagement and an increasing commitment to peace-keeping and support for humanitarian tasks. This presence of Europe in the world has acted as a stabilising force in many regions and created an awareness in other parts of the world of the usefulness of the European model.

In other continents, such as Latin America, Africa and Asia, groups of countries struggle with great difficulty to follow in the footsteps of the EU. In these regions, governments are working to establish common customs unions and free trade areas. They are taking the first tentative steps along a road that the EU travelled many years ago.

Fourthly, and most importantly, Europe has proceeded not solely on the basis of a grand plan or vision but by a careful step-by-step approach built around strong and representative institutions. The European institutions – in particular, the Commission, the Parliament and the European Court of Justice – have served the Union well. The existence of powerful, fair and neutral institutions has ensured that Europe has developed on the basis of equality amongst the Member States. The failure to develop these detailed treaties and strong institutions would have seen Europe inevitably develop into a political entity where one or other group of Member States held dominance over others. Such an approach would have been fatal, either in the short or medium term, to the entire project. The very essence of the European Union has been built on consent and consensus. Such an approach is of course time-consuming. Such an approach is inherently difficult. Such an approach will inevitably meet setbacks along the way. However, as time-consuming as this approach to building Europe is, it is the only one that will work.

It is in all of our interests, both as citizens and as Member States, that this step-by-step approach to building Europe continues. For it is a fact that the challenges facing the individual Member States today are of such magnitude that even the largest state on its own will not be able to meet these challenges effectively. Climate change, globalisation, international crime and the development of the poorest countries are issues that can be tackled only by states working together. The European Union is the most effective example of this cooperative approach.

Following the rejection of the European Constitution in the referenda held in France and The Netherlands many of the comments in the media have been extremely pessimistic as to the future of Europe. However, it is important to keep a sense of perspective. The reality is that since the fall of the Iron Curtain the European Union has experienced unprecedented growth. It has more than doubled its membership. It has created a single currency. It has greatly enhanced its single market. The key challenge for Europe following the referenda results is to maintain the momentum of that success. Europe in this context faces a number of real challenges.

Firstly, the European Union needs to upgrade its institutional framework. The structures of the European Union were designed for six Member States. It is difficult to see how they could effectively function, in the medium to long-term, in a Union of twenty-eight or thirty Member States. This is why the members agreed the new European Constitution. The Constitution is a good document, a document Ireland would like to see enacted as soon as possible.

Obviously, the rejection of the Treaty by the voters of France and The Netherlands, two of the founding members of the Union, is a setback in the ratification process. The Treaty will not now come into force by the target date of November 2006.

In June 2005, the European Council discussed the situation and decided that it was necessary to have a pause for reflection. The European Council did not rush to hasty conclusions about the reasons for the French and Dutch rejection of the Constitution. It agreed that the process of ratification of the European Constitution remained valid. In fact, since June 2005, three further countries have ratified the Constitution.

The European Council agreed that, during the pause in the ratification process, each country should have a broad debate about Europe involving all relevant sections of society. The European Council will assess these national debates during the Austrian Presidency in the first half of 2006 and decide how to proceed.

I want our national debate to be open, constructive and inclusive. The National Forum for Europe will take the lead in facilitating the contributions from all sections of society. To inform the discussion, the Government has published a comprehensive information booklet setting out our national goals and objectives in the European Union in the coming year (Department of the Taoiseach, 2005).

Since the French and Dutch referenda, there has been much talk in the EU of bringing the EU closer to the people. There have been calls for a stronger role for national parliaments in the EU legislative process, for less intrusiveness and less regulation from the EU Commission, for a more efficient, effective and accountable Union.

The EU Member States who have not had a great deal of experience in managing national referenda have been taken aback to find that many voters do not have a positive view of the Union. Many voters are poorly informed about developments in the Union over the past decade. Many see the Union as remote from their daily concerns. They are increasingly exasperated by over-regulation. They have questions about the accountability of the institutions of the Union.

Because of our difficult national debate during the two referenda on the Nice Treaty, we in Ireland were one of the first to identify this sense of disconnection between the people and the EU as a serious European problem that needed to be addressed. We have worked to address it through the National Forum on Europe, through revitalised Oireachtas scrutiny of EU legislation and through the Government's Communicating Europe Initiative.[2]

In the debates taking place in the Member States, we in Europe must reject soundly the voices of those who want us to return to the past. Nowhere is this more the case than in Ireland. There are many who want to stand on the beach and tell the tide of globalisation to turn back on itself, go away and leave them in peace. We have heard their voices before. In 1972, they said that joining the EU would be the economic ruin of Ireland. In the five referenda we have had since 1972 they said that acceptance of the Single European Act, of the Treaty of Maastricht, of the Treaty of Amsterdam and of the Treaty of Nice would see the end of Ireland's sovereignty and our absorption into a European superstate where we would have no voice. They were wrong then. They are wrong now.

As a country, Ireland is now more successful, more confident and more optimistic than at any time since the foundation of the State. We are a country transformed. And our EU membership has played a vital role in this transformation. We must not forget this. We must not take it for granted. We need to continue to work hard as a country not only to promote and protect our national interests in the EU but also, and equally importantly, to work for the success of the Union as whole. A weak and divided Europe is not in Ireland's national interest. A Europe beset by doubt and losing faith in its vision is not in Ireland's interest.

Secondly, Europe faces the challenge of making enlargement work and of continuing the enlargement process. We have made a good start with the enlargement of May 2004 when ten new Member States joined; these countries are adapting rapidly and effectively to the Union. It is essential that we reach an early agreement on the future financing of the Union to ensure that these Member States receive

WHERE DOES THE EUROPEAN UNION GO NOW?

adequate funding with a view to narrowing the income gaps between new and old Member States.

The years of work that resulted in the agreement on the European Constitution were not inspired by an excess of zeal to promote European integration. This work was not promoted by an out-of-touch elite. It was inspired by recognition of the simple fact that the unification of Europe after the Cold War has changed forever the continent and the Union. And this is an enormously positive change. It is also a change which underlines the immensely important role of the Union as an anchor of peace, stability and democracy on a continent that is still adjusting to the ending of the Cold War.

This stabilising role of the Union remains central to the future political and economic development of the continent. The European Constitution sets out the Union's values – respect for human dignity, freedom, democracy, equality, the rule of law and respect for human rights, including the rights of persons belonging to minorities. The Constitution also provides that membership of the Union is open to all European states which respect these values.

It was on this basis that the ten new Member States joined the EU. Similarly, we look forward to the accession of Bulgaria and Romania, expected in 2007.

I have always believed that the expansion of the Union should be accompanied by measures to ensure that a wider Union does not mean a looser Union. In my view, enlargement is not a cover for turning the Union into a looser entity more akin to a trade bloc. That is why the European Constitution is so important. It will ensure that the enlargement of the Union to twenty-five and beyond will take place in a legal framework which guarantees the Union's political character and enables the Member States to continue to take decisions effectively and in the interests of all. And that is why rigorous standards must be met before accession can take place. The ten new Member States, like earlier acceding states, including Ireland, have had to make enormous efforts and real sacrifices to obtain membership.

This is one of the reasons the European Union has succeeded. While compromise is an essential lubricant of its day-to-day operation, there has never been room for compromise on the essential prerequisites of respect for democracy, the rule of law and the ground rules of the European Union itself.

Thirdly, we need to make Europe work economically for all its citizens. It is a source of great concern to all that the core economies of Europe have not performed as well as they could over recent years. While the launch of the single currency has been a tremendous success, the ongoing sluggish growth and high unemployment in the core euro economies has played a major part in dampening public ardour for the European project. The solution to these economic problems lies largely in the hands of national governments rather than at EU level. It is essential, however, that Europe continues to build a common understanding and approach to the economic challenges facing it in the coming years.

We need to have both a national and an EU-wide discussion about the European Union and globalisation. To the world outside the Union, the EU is a powerful and integrated economic bloc. This enables the Union to promote and defend the interests of all the Member States in crucial global trade negotiations in the World Trade Organisation.

While the EU is dealing effectively with the process of globalisation on the international stage, the Union has not yet fully come to terms with globalisation internally. Among the twenty-five, we too often behave as if competition between the Member States is a challenge on a level with the competition we face externally from China, from India and from Brazil. We have not yet fully grasped the fact that the full realisation of the EU's internal market will be a source of immense strength for the Union. We do not always understand that the success of any one Member State in attracting major mobile internal investment is a success for all of us. We underestimate the Union's potential. We have failed to fully harness the economic and social benefits that should flow from the internal market, from our common currency and from collective action in research and development.

Clearly, one of the key factors influencing voters in France and The Netherlands was economic uncertainty and fears for the future. There is, however, a danger that the debate about how best the EU can face up to the competitive challenge of globalisation will be sidetracked into a fruitless discussion about the relative merits of different social models. The simple fact is that the principal levers of economic change and economic reform remain in the hands of the Member States. While at the level of the Union we can encourage, we can coordinate, we can advise, we can apply peer pressure, the key decisions remain with the Member States.

There is, quite rightly, no uniform social model that is applicable to all of the Member States. Throughout the EU, however, there is, in contrast to much of the rest of the developed world, a high degree of social solidarity and a strong commitment to balancing the forces of the market with the protection of workers' rights. While there may be differences of emphasis, I believe that there is no deep division between the different social systems of the Member States.

What the EU needs is to focus on those areas where, acting together, we can ensure that the enlarged Union of 460 million people remains a global trade and economic power and a strong partner to the developing world. This means that we should focus our energies on completing the internal market, including the market in services. It means that we should have a well-developed and coherent strategy for managing our overall relationship with China and the other rising economies. It means that we should have a clear and proactive approach to dealing with the economic and social dislocations that globalisation brings in its wake. This requires a strong dialogue with the social partners. It requires EU investments in research and development, in retraining and the development of new skills, in active labour market policies.

What the EU needs, therefore, is an agreed collective approach to the challenge of globalisation. Acting together, using all of the resources, the institutions, the powers and the policies we have agreed at EU level, we can support one another in facing up to the challenges of globalisation.

Finally, I strongly believe our national debate should focus also on Ireland's relationship with the EU. Much has been written about the influence of our EU membership on the political, economic, social and cultural development of Ireland. However, over the past decade both Ireland and the Union have changed dramatically. For much of our membership, Ireland was one of the less well off Member States of the EU, with per capita income in the majority of Member States significantly in excess of ours. During that period, Ireland benefited greatly from Structural and Cohesion Funds.

In the years to come, however, Ireland will gradually become a net contributor to the EU budget. We will pay into the EU more than we receive back. This progression should be seen as a mark of our success as an economy and of our commitment to ensuring that the less well off Member States, particularly the new Member States, receive the same support from the EU that was of such benefit to us.

As our status in the EU changes, we will adapt accordingly our national policy approach to issues on the day-to-day EU agenda to reflect our changing interests. We will, for example, take a much closer interest in areas of the EU budget, such as research and development expenditure, which correspond to our national priorities.

We will also have to adapt the way in which we communicate with the public about our EU membership. Up to now, much of the message to our people about the benefits of EU membership has understandably focused on the direct financial benefit to Ireland. In the years to come, we will have to focus more on the indirect benefits of membership, such as the importance of direct access to the EU's internal market for the hundreds of thousands of people employed in industry and services. We will also have to do more to inform people about the political significance of the Union, about its role in promoting peace and stability in Europe and about how, through our EU membership, we have a voice in major global issues.

During this period of reflection, I would like to encourage greater public understanding and awareness of the reasons why our EU membership is, and will remain, of fundamental importance to our national prosperity even when we no longer benefit greatly from direct EU financial transfers.

When we consider this issue, it is critically important to look at the values for which the EU stands and how they reflect our national values. The EU is a profound force for good both in the continent of Europe and in the wider world. In a world which is grappling with globalisation, confronting terrorism, facing the challenge of climate change, struggling to resolve difficult regional conflicts and where over one billion people still live in extreme poverty, it is in our interests to be in a Union which shares our fundamental values.

I think that if we focus on issues such as the EU and globalisation, on the EU and enlargement and on Ireland's changing status in a changing Union, the discussion will rightly and inevitably return again and again to the European Constitution. The challenges facing the Union in the new Europe, and in a rapidly changing world, compel us to give a definitive answer to the question that has been on the EU's agenda for many years, namely, what is the end point of EU integration?

The European Constitution is the answer to this question. It provides the legal and institutional framework for the enlarged Union to act effectively in the interests of all its citizens. It resolves the debate about the relationship between the Union and the Member States for at least a generation. It will allow us to get on with the work of providing jobs, fighting crime, protecting the environment, resolving conflict and helping poor and underdeveloped countries.

Notes

1. This paper was presented at the conference, *The Future of Europe: Uniting Vision, Values and Citizens?*, held in Dublin on 27 September 2005.
2. The Communicating Europe Initiative was established by the Irish Government in 1995 to provide Irish people with information on developments and events in the European Union. It is managed by the European Union Division of the Department of Foreign Affairs.

Reference

Department of the Taoiseach (2005) *Ireland and the European Union: Identifying Priorities and Pursuing Goals*, third edition, Dublin.

Europe

Identity, Convergence and Expansion[1]

Peter Sutherland

In his seminal speech on European integration in the University of
Zurich on 19 September 1946, Winston Churchill spoke of the old
continent as being 'united in the sharing of its common inheritance'. He
portrayed the base of Greco–Roman culture and Christian faith and
ethics as being 'at the origin of most of the culture, arts, philosophy and
science both of ancient and modern times'. But it was our conflicts
rather than our similarities that really motivated him. His recognition of
shared roots presumed everyone in that lecture hall knew that he saw the
nationalistic struggles that had 'wrecked the peace and marred the
prospects of mankind' as the real reason for his desire to see 'a United
States of Europe' (albeit one from which Great Britain would stand
somewhat apart). Certainly, it was the agonies of divisive histories rather
than any sense of a shared European identity that drove the founding
fathers of the European Union, such as Robert Schuman, Konrad
Adenauer, Alcide De Gasperi and Paul-Henri Spaak, to propose a new
institutional structure to help reconciliation and future peace. There
were, of course, other reasons motivating them, such as the rejection of
what one observer has described as: 'The false universalism of
communism and the false particularism of fascism, one of which sought
to make everyone the same and the other of which refused any sense of
common humanity'.

Those times are now long past and the context of our present
debate is different. The threat of fratricidal conflict in Europe has
receded and our peoples seem, perhaps complacently, unconcerned by
it. Moreover, apart from the faltering memories of past conflicts, we
no longer have the need to be cemented together in mutual protection
against Russia and its allies.

So, inevitably, attitudes to European integration, particularly
among the young, have changed and are challenged by new realities

such as the enlargement of the EU. Belief in the process of integration can no longer be promoted by the recollections of terrible events now within the living memory of only a small and diminishing minority. We must, therefore, rethink and restate the case for European integration. This will be assisted by an understanding that the fundamental relationship between the nation state and the citizen has been changed in the globalising and increasingly interdependent world of today. Of course, it had been the nation state, and the manner in which it functioned, particularly since the nineteenth century, that had created many of our historic problems. In 1826 the British Foreign Secretary, George Canning, remarked, following the collapse of the Congress of Vienna system: 'Things are getting back to a wholesome state, every nation for itself, and God for us all.' His world was that which many of us hope we have escaped fearing, as President Mitterand said in his farewell speech to the European Parliament, *'Le nationalism, c'est la guerre'*.

So what is this concept of a nation state which some eurosceptics, and nationalists in particular, wish to retain? It means different things to different people. Jeremy Rifkin has written: 'The popular conception of the Nation State ... is rooted in common culture, language and customs. [But] in reality [it] is more of ... an artificial construct ...' (Rifkin, 2004, p. 166) Often, in order to create it, it was necessary, he wrote, to 'create a compelling story about a common past, one convincing enough to capture the imagination of the people and convince them of their shared identity and common destiny'. The reality is often more complex. There are, indeed, shared histories and values, and the binding together of communities has many valid and positive aspects that are not contrived. It has to be admitted, however, that in many cases the alleged unity of peoples has been a recent phenomenon and is less than fully convincing historically. National languages have been important in this but, for example, in 1789 less than 50 per cent of the French people spoke French and in 1861 only 2 per cent of Italians spoke Italian. Castilian was very much a minority language in Spain. After the Reformation, religion too had an effect in creating a sense of a shared past and a common destiny for majorities in a national state, although it also has had the divisive effect of creating a question mark over the nationality of minorities. However, the fact is that most people in Europe feel an intense and often passionate sense of belonging to a nation state. This could never be supplanted by a European identity, nor should it be. It is to national identity that people primarily cling. The Danish intellectual, Toger Seidenfaden, wrote:

> There is no European people, no European ethnicity, no European demos ... as a consequence the EU is notoriously incapable of generating popular enthusiasm on any major scale. This is, of course, one of its most attractive features.

Whilst this comment goes a little too far for my taste, one can see what he meant.

Ernest Renan has written that the nation is a spiritual principle consisting of two things: 'a common legacy of rich memories from the past and a consensus to forget the oppressions and injustices that once divided the members of the nation.' (Renan, 1882) We have all seen this in action. Most Europeans today probably see themselves as part of one race or another, although their DNA may well provide evidence of a more complex reality. Unfortunately, many probably see their race as being essentially 'better' than others, at least in some respects. This is part of the legacy of nationalism and perhaps the price for the cohesion of a community. Of course, too, there are confusing overlaps between nations within nations. Examples proliferate around Europe. The British are comprised of a group of perceived nationalities, as are the Spanish and many others. The question as to where their ultimate loyalty lies would be hard to answer for many a Scot, a Walloon, a Bavarian or a Catalan.

In his book, *Europe: A History*, Norman Davies (1996) draws a distinction between civilisation and culture. The former is defined as: 'the sum total of ideas and traditions which had been inherited from the ancient world and from Christianity.' In other words, it constitutes what binds us together. Culture, on the other hand, is seen by him as growing 'from the everyday life of the people ... In earlier times civilisation was extolled and culture despised. Nationalism did the opposite'.

All of this makes for a volatile situation, particularly when one takes into account the new challenges of integrating the relatively recent waves of migrants from within Europe itself and also from outside, particularly north Africa. We now have a Europe that is increasingly diversified within its component parts with, for example, its population including ten million Muslims. Paradoxically, too, while the EU integrates nation states with each other, it also can create the seeds of national disintegration. This is because nation states that contain different ethnic strands were often bound together in the past because of the advantages of economic integration within a nation state, combined with the need for protection from external aggression. Neither of these conditions exists today within the EU. Essentially, the completion of the common market and the ending of the prospect of intra-European warfare have removed the fears that formerly drove regions to adhere to a larger nation state. Many Catalan or Basque nationalists, for example, see little point in a continued connection with Madrid if it costs them money. Furthermore, a positive reason for division into smaller units is that, within the EU, there is increasing evidence of greater economic success amongst the smaller nation states than the larger. The three highest levels of GDP per capita are to be found in Luxembourg, Ireland and Denmark. This is argued by some to be influenced by the greater flexibility in domestic economic policy that each can now deploy. These smaller states can adapt to the opportunities afforded by full access to a vast common market in a more focused and effective way than larger states.

So, today, our political structures have to accommodate a series of apparently conflicting realities. These include separatism and integration, diversity and shared values. The EU can help in this accommodation. We have to build upon and develop our shared values to bind us together, whilst not attempting to stifle the legitimate distinctions and loyalties between ethnic or religious groups within our collective body politic. If we do not maintain a sense of some shared identity and interdependence we will be unable to continue to justify the essential supranational aspects of what the EU is. As William Wallace, the political scientist, wrote in the early 1980s of the then European Community, it is 'less than a federation, more than a regime'. (Wallace, 1983) This is particularly the case because, within agreed confines, laws can be made that are opposed by individual Member States and the direct effect of EU law makes national law and national courts less than fully sovereign.

The integration process should help to develop a common political community to protect the values, political diversity, democracy and human rights in which we jointly believe and which will act as a defence against the attack on any of these at national level. The EU should, in a broader sense too, be the means for the resolution of the 'contradictions of tribalism and globalism' (Horsman and Marshall, 1995). We are assisted in this because we are much more alike today than many recognise. Indeed, on the big issues of our time, European peoples are remarkably united in attitudes that reflect their shared values. Their distinctive positions can be contrasted with those currently prevailing in other parts of the world, including the United States. In this regard Robert Kagan has detailed our differences. Although his description of a Europe of Kant's perpetual peace, as against a Hobbesian US defending and promoting a liberal order through force, is a gross simplification, it reflects some truth. We believe in communitarianism, solidarity and multilateralism in a specific European way. The fact that, according to Eurobarometer surveys, Europeans, in a majority everywhere, want 'a more independent' common foreign and defence policy is a reflection of an increasing European belief that we share more in our approaches to international affairs with our European neighbours than anything that divides us. That was shown in reactions to the Iraq war, where public opinion was generally negative to the war throughout the EU, even though European leaders were notoriously divided, with some courting unpopularity in supporting the US. On the domestic front,

30

too, we share similar views on a wide range of issues – from, for example, the death penalty to the extent and limitations of individual freedom. The European convergence means that we and others now have a capacity to work together to constructively influence a world full of both opportunities and threats. If we fail to do so together even the largest states will reduce their influence over their own destiny and the distinctive European viewpoint will be increasingly marginalised and ignored internationally.

In my opinion, the approach of the current leadership of some important Member States to global challenges facing the EU has regrettably been to retreat towards national capitals rather than advance the integration process that we need to deal with the issues of interdependence. Should it persist, this will gradually undermine institutions such as the European Commission and the European Parliament, both having a limited but clear federal vocation. The 'No' votes in France and The Netherlands have been interpreted incorrectly as votes against European integration and this may increase this inter-governmentalist tendency. They have also been interpreted by some as a warning against further enlargement, particularly with regard to Turkey.

Let me turn now to the issue of future enlargements and possible limits to the expansion of the EU, having regard to this issue of shared identity. Firstly, however, it should be emphasised that the enlargement of the EU can no longer be considered as inevitable, even for those countries within Europe that comply with the requirements set in what are known as 'the Copenhagen Criteria'. There is the likelihood that, in the future, new accessions will take place only after specific referenda in at least some existing Member States. It needs to be recognised in particular, too, that amongst those most likely to oppose enlargement to include Turkey will be some committed integrationalists who argue that Turkish membership damages the cohesion of the EU.

The debate about Turkish accession, therefore, crystallises many of the questions about identity, history, attitudes and values within the EU. Religion plays a real part in this. Even though the founding fathers of the EU were virtually all Christian Democrats, they did not invoke God or Christianity as a factor in European integration. Indeed, the separation of Church and State remained the prevailing position in the conclusion of the debate on the Constitutional Treaty. Yet, Christianity is the heritage of many Europeans. Article 1–52 of the Constitution states: 'The Union respects and does not prejudice the status under national law of churches and religious associations or communities in the Member States.' However, an invocation of God in the Preamble was omitted (although only after fierce debate during which Catholics were joined by Lutheran, Calvinist and Orthodox Churches). One can take it, however, as evidenced by the papal blessing of the politicians who convened in Rome on 29 October 2004 to sign the Constitutional Treaty, that the Catholic Church, for example, did not reject the draft. However, this accepted division between the Church and State in the EU does not mean that there are no objections to Turkish accession based upon a perception that the Turkish people are in some sense different and this is connected with religion. Thus, although Pope John Paul II (2003) in *Ecclesia in Europa* (n. 111) made the point that, 'Saying "Europe" must be the equivalent to saying "openness"', it is apparent that this openness has limitations. Pope Benedict XVI is publicly against Turkish accession. He is not, of course, alone in this. The President of the Convention on the Future of Europe, Giscard d'Estaing, has said that Turkish accession would mean, 'the end of the EU'. Nor is the accession supported by President Chirac, German Chancellor, Angela Merkel or Chancellor Schussel of Austria and these politicians, amongst others, clearly reflect the views of many Europeans.

It may be asked whether this opposition is related to questions surrounding the distinctive identity and values of the Turkish people or whether it is simply related to more pragmatic concerns such as the fear of migration, the lack of development of the Turkish economy or questions about the real depth of its democracy. It might also specifically relate to the treatment of religion in Turkey. Olli Rehn, the European Commissioner for Enlargement has said, 'freedom of religion is one of the key issues to be addressed by Turkey'. The reality is that the debates about secularism in Turkey today, such as whether to make adultery a criminal offence or whether boys who have been to religious schools can pursue a university education of their choosing, underline the fact that should the accession of Turkey occur it will create a very new and much deeper diversity in the EU.

In any case, there is an existing commitment to negotiations. These will take many years to conclude and only then will it be possible to judge whether Turkey could or should be a full member. That judgement will depend, in turn, on a fair assessment of the extent to which Turkey can subscribe to a deepening political integration founded upon shared values and the attitudes that emanate from them.

The very fact that this debate is taking place now, whatever its merits, underlines the existence of a widely-shared belief that there is something distinctive and important in European values and attitudes and that the EU is about more than the creation of a functioning market supported by some elements of cross-border solidarity.

Even though the Constitution has not been adopted, it presents, in its terms, a reasonable template for our future development. Article 1–1 was exhaustively discussed and it simply states that any European country that subscribes to promoting the Union's values is eligible for accession. It did not define what it is meant by 'European' but it is a geographic concept that has been interpreted to include states that are potentially within the border of the continent. The values are set out in Article 1–2:

> The Union is founded on the values of respect for human dignity, freedom, equality, democracy, the rule of law and respect for human rights, including the rights of persons belonging to minorities. These values are common to the Member States in a society in which pluralism, non-discrimination, tolerance, justice, solidarity and equality between women and men prevail.

The objectives of the European Union, set out in Article 1–3, state that the Union shall 'promote economic, social and territorial cohesion among Member States' and 'respect for its rich cultural and linguistic diversity', and shall also 'ensure that Europe's cultural heritage is safeguarded and enhanced'. These all seem to be an expression of identity that has a real meaning.

I believe that the meaning of these values and objectives have a particular – and shared – European interpretation. It is not intended to be divisive or disparaging to suggest that this interpretation is different to that applied in other parts of the world. Our cultures may be distinct but our development has gradually brought us together in a unique way, which we can build upon. The late Hugo Young once wrote in *The Guardian* about our European cultures: 'It is helpful to learn that there are not rival cultures, a zero sum game of allegiance, but that they mingled and grew together.' We should seek to continue that process of growing together.

Note

1. This paper was presented at the conference, *The Future of Europe: Uniting Vision, Values and Citizens?*, held in Dublin on 27 September 2005.

References

Davies, Norman (1996) *Europe: A History*, Oxford: Oxford University Press.

Horsmann, Mathew and Andrew Marshall (1995) *After the Nation-state: Citizens, Tribalism and the New World Order*, London: HarperCollins.

Pope John Paul II (2003) *Ecclesia in Europa*, Post-Synodial Apostolic Exhortation, 28 June 2003.

Renan, Ernest (1882) 'What is a Nation?' in Geoff Eley and Ronald Grigor Suny (1996) (eds) *Becoming National: A Reader*, New York and Oxford: Oxford University Press.

Rifkin, Jeremy (2004) *The European Dream: How Europe's Vision of the Future is Quietly Eclipsing the American Dream*, Cambridge: Polity Press.

Wallace, William (1983) 'Less than a Federation, More than a Regime: the Community as Political System', in Helen Wallace, William Wallace and Carole Webb (eds) *Policy-Making in the European Community*, second edition, London: John Wiley and Sons, pp. 403–6.

The Future of Europe

Challenges for Faith and Values[1]

Diarmuid Martin

> If we look at Europe as a civil community, *signs of hope* are not
> lacking: when we consider these signs with the eyes of faith, we
> can perceive, even amid the contradictions of history, the
> presence of the Spirit of God, who renews the face of the earth.
> (Pope John Paul II, 2003, n. 12)

These are the remarkably strong words of Pope John Paul II about
the European endeavour, from his letter, *Ecclesia in Europa*. Pope
John Paul was indeed an extraordinary European. I always
remember the first time I heard him explicitly state his view that the
decisions of Yalta were unjust and had to be reviewed. At that point,
this was heresy; it was as politically incorrect as you could get at the
time. Yalta, no matter how undesirable, was a fact of *realpolitik* and
to challenge it – according to the accepted wisdom – was to put the
stability of Europe at risk.

Even the Helsinki process – which played an enormous role in the
promotion and protection of human rights right across Europe – set
out from the presumption that there would be no changes in the
boundaries of the European states. In the diplomatic language of the
times, that effectively meant that the regimes of eastern Europe – in
particular, the German Democratic Republic – would remain for
much time to come. It is amusing to see the list of those who signed
the Helsinki agreements. The signatures of all the old party chiefs and
dictators of eastern Europe are there; quite a motley crew! I will not
comment on the names of the western side.

Pope John Paul II was always led by the inspiration that a different
Europe was possible. This was similar to the insight of the founders of
the European Communities who went against what was, for centuries,
the politically correct praxis that at the end of a war the loser was to

be punished. They, inspired by their Christian faith, looked to a vision which stressed that, in the long term, the future of Europe depended not on punishing or isolating but on integrating.

The Gift of Peace

These two changes in European geography and politics – the process of the establishment of the European Union and the move to true democracy in the countries of central and eastern Europe – have produced that great gift which was so lacking in the Europe of the twentieth century: peace. European nationalism had given rise in the twentieth century to the two most disastrous wars of human history. We cannot forget the horror of the fighting in the trenches of the First World War, and the stories of children falsifying their age to be enrolled. Europe – with the exclusion of the Balkans – has now not seen war for over sixty years. Nations that for centuries had been enemies have found a peaceful working relationship. This is an enormous achievement and we thank God for it.

It should not be forgotten that in addition to the European Union, there was another movement of integration in Europe after the Second World War and that was NATO. Many think of NATO as just an anti-communist phalanx. NATO, however, was also built on the principle of integration. It aimed at keeping the military powers of Europe integrated and not allowing any one of them to remilitarise to the detriment of others. It should also be remembered that after the fall of the communist systems, the desire of the central and eastern European governments to integrate into a new Europe meant joining NATO just as much as joining the European Union. They knew that at a perilous moment for their security, security would only be defended through participation in an alliance that included the United States. This realisation of how their security was linked with a North Atlantic alliance might also explain to some degree the greater willingness of the central and eastern European countries to support the United States on other occasions.

European Consciousness, Identity and Values

Where is Europe going today? What are the signs of hope? What are the signs which should cause us concern? On what principles will the Europe of the future base its values? What will be the contribution of faith and of men and women of faith to the construction of those values?

Pope John Paul II, in *Ecclesia in Europa*, was moderately optimistic and hopeful in his analysis of some of the developments in Europe in recent years. Taking up the reflections of the First and Second Special Assemblies for Europe of the Synod of Bishops (1991 and 1999), he indicated some of these positive aspects.

The first was one to which I have already alluded, namely reconciliation between countries which had been hostile and the progressive opening to the counties of eastern Europe. This, in its turn, has led to what Pope John Paul called the creation of a European consciousness. This concept and culture of Europe, the Pope would note, draws from the fact that:

> More than a geographical area, Europe can be described as a *primarily cultural and historical concept*, which denotes a reality born as a continent thanks also to the unifying force of Christianity, which has been capable of integrating people and cultures among themselves ... (n. 108)

The idea of a European consciousness was taken up in a talk given in 1991 by the then Cardinal Joseph Ratzinger, now Pope Benedict XVI, who spoke of 'the prestige of the idea of Europe'. Ratzinger pointed out that the ideal had seen its high point at the hour of necessity, when nationalism, elevated to an ideological barrier, had shattered the nations of the old continent. It is interesting that after the horrors of each of the two world wars there was a clear understanding that peace required some concept of collective security which would curb exaggerated nationalism. Thus, after the First World War came the idea of the League of Nations, which sadly rapidly became the victim of the lack of coherence of its own member states. After the Second

World War, the United Nations emerged on a world level and the idea of European unification took on a new chapter in its history. But Ratzinger also noted that in our day the ideal of Europe had become blunted. He noted that the Europe of the future must recover its links to its 'common roots, the common civilisation built up on multiple exchanges, on the common moral and religious heritage, on the rational character of that civilisation and of its creative force for unity'.[2] For Ratzinger, a European culture is one which stresses what unifies and what is common over and above all division.

Pope John Paul II and his successor Pope Benedict XVI are thus both convinced Europeans. This springs from their personal experience of the tragic consequences of extreme nationalism and the effects on society when fundamental values break down. But this does not mean that they embrace any vision of Europe or that they are not aware of 'the contradictions of history' or are uncritical of certain current expressions of the European ideal.

Pope John Paul noted clearly that:

> Today's Europe, however, at the very moment that it is in the process of strengthening and enlarging its economic and political union, seems to suffer from a profound crisis of values. While possessed of increased resources, it gives the impression of lacking the energy needed to sustain a common project and to give its citizen new reasons for hope. (n. 108)

Further, he notes: 'In the process of transformation which it is now undergoing, *Europe is called above all to re-discover its true identity.*' (n. 109) In the light of the crisis of European identity which has emerged around the project of the draft Constitutional Treaty, these words of Pope John Paul were clearly to the point.

European Union Constitutional Treaty

In *Ecclesia in Europa*, Pope John Paul made a direct appeal to those who at the time were drawing up the Constitutional Treaty of the

European Union, as he had done in speaking to the Diplomatic Corps accredited to the Holy See earlier in 2003. It is useful to recall exactly what Pope John Paul asked for. In the first place, he asked that the Treaty contain 'a reference to the religious and in particular the Christian heritage of Europe' (n. 114). This request was answered in part. There is reference – despite the initial objection of some countries – to the religious heritage, but not explicitly to the Christian heritage. The text does refer to the contribution of Churches to the construction of Europe – and only Christians have Churches!

It is useful to recall that the rejection of this appeal for an explicit mention of the Christian heritage of Europe was not some sort of a pan-European plot against religion, but *de facto* the result of the rigid and immovable objection principally of one European nation.

Pope John Paul then made a further appeal that three complementary elements be recognised in the Treaty. These were:

> ... the right of Churches and religious communities to organize themselves freely in conformity with their statutes and proper convictions; respect for the specific identity of the different religious confessions and provision for a structured dialogue between the European Union and those confessions; and respect for the juridical status already enjoyed by Churches and religious institutions by virtue of the legislation of the Member States of the Union. (n. 114)

Effectively, the Constitution incorporated these suggestions.

In *Ecclesia in Europa*, Pope John Paul did not make an explicit request for the inclusion of a mention of God in the Constitutional Treaty.

Human Rights and their Interpretation

Pope John Paul did mention a further series of values or focal points of value which the Union should address. One was respect for human rights, of individuals, minorities and peoples. The European Union considers respect for human rights as a fundamental foundational principle of its existence and policy. The difficulty here is to understand what is covered under the term 'human rights' and where human rights are grounded, especially in a period where juridical culture is dominated in Europe and elsewhere by legal positivism and by individualism. Whereas these trends are not exclusive to the European Union, the Union has become a powerful vehicle for the propagation of a certain interpretation of human rights.

This applies in particular to the right to life from the moment of its conception to natural death and to the family based on marriage. There is no doubt that decisions of both political and juridical organs of the European Union can be greatly influenced by ideological visions, but again it is often the case that these visions are present due to the strong influence of individual Member States, which at times look on such an understanding of human rights as part of national policy.

It is true that the viewpoint of the Church enjoys a stronger adherence within the culture of some individual states than in the Union itself and it is feared that the European Union structures might be used to undermine such national cultures. In other cases, the national juridical culture is even more liberal than that of the Union. In any case, recent events show that, with or without a European Union, individual countries can overnight radically change their policy on issues such as those of marriage and family.

There should be a greater alertness on the national level – both within government and within civil society – in monitoring mechanisms of the Union if they push to a standardisation of issues and values which perhaps goes beyond the specific competence or mandate of the Union itself. It is important to monitor also what is done through the interaction of the EU Member States in the field of multilateral diplomacy.

The structures of the European Union still have a democratic deficit, although efforts are being made to remedy this. In the interim period, not only are strong monitoring mechanisms required to identify over-reach of competence but there is a need to push for a priority option for subsidiarity rather than for centralisation, a priority option for what has been democratically established over the power of non-elected bureaucrats.

Openness, Solidarity and Global Justice

There is a further striking short sentence of Pope John Paul in *Ecclesia in Europa*. The Pope says: 'Saying "Europe" must be equivalent to saying "openness"'. (n. 111) This means that any European vision must be one based on openness and that Europe must respond with justice and equity and a great sense of solidarity (n. 111). Pope John Paul then quotes from his October 2000 letter to Cardinal Miloslav Vlk, President of the Council of European Episcopal Conferences:

> Europe cannot close in on itself. It cannot and must not lose interest in the rest of the world. On the contrary, it must remain fully aware of the fact that other countries, other continents, await its bold initiatives, in order to offer to poorer peoples the means for their growth and social organization, and to build a more just and fraternal world. (n. 111)

And quoting from his Message for the 2000 Day of Peace, Pope John Paul goes on to speak of the importance of *'rethinking international cooperation in terms of a new culture of solidarity'*:

> When seen as a sowing of peace, cooperation cannot be reduced to aid or assistance, especially if given with an eye to the benefits to be received in return for the resources made available. Rather, it must express a concrete and tangible commitment to solidarity which makes the poor the agents of their own development and enables the greatest number of people, in their specific economic and political circumstances, to exercise the creativity which is characteristic of the human person and on which the wealth of nations too is dependent. (n. 111)

There is a sense in which a Europe based on the concept of integration can never be satisfied within its own boundaries. Its sense of responsibility at least must be always outward looking. This does not mean that it can just embrace every country as a member and that it must open its borders indiscriminately to all. European Union expansion is a complex matter. Studies have shown that those countries of central and eastern Europe which have been most successful in their search to become modern, democratic nations with a flourishing free market are those which had to go through the exercise of adapting to the norms of EU integration. The process itself has its own value. Other states, which have not been accepted for membership by the EU, have been slower and more lax in the process of modernisation. There is no short-cut along the path of the economic and democratic reforms needed to join the European Union.

Europe has responsibilities worldwide. I have said on many occasions that it is not the task of the European Union to become a 'mini superpower', but to be maxi and super in its spirit of solidarity. Again, I quote Pope John Paul: 'Europe must moreover become *an active partner in promoting and implementing a globalization "in" solidarity.*' (n. 112) There is, however, a growing tendency on the part of the EU in international negotiations to adopt some of the trappings of a superpower, especially in trade negotiations. Of course, once again, the EU positions in trade negotiations, especially in agriculture and textiles and intellectual property rights, are very often subject to pressure from national governments and national interest groups. The Union is often held back from more enlightened positions by national interest.

The Role of Christians

What is the role of Christians in forming the new Europe? The first thing is that they be present, that they bring their voice to the table and ensure that it is heard. *Ecclesia in Europa* stresses that 'Europe needs a *religious dimension.*' (n. 116) And again, 'Europe needs to make a qualitative leap in *becoming conscious of its spiritual heritage.*' (n. 120).

This task should be undertaken with renewed vigour – and also in an ecumenical context – by the Church as an institution and by individual Christians exercising their mission as lay persons in the structures of society.

It may not be the task of the European institutions themselves to build that religious dimension, but they should ensure that mechanisms are there to facilitate the contribution of religion and of believers and not become an obstacle. It is to be hoped that the proposals of this nature outlined in the draft Constitutional Treaty will find concrete expression, independent of whatever the fate of the entire draft Treaty may be.

The Gospel can elicit a new enthusiasm within Europe and bring a message of hope. All European Christians can make a contribution to this process. In *Ecclesia in Europa*, Pope John Paul quotes from his letter of October 2000 to the President of the Council of European Episcopal Conferences:

> Not only can Christians join with all people of goodwill in working to build this great project, but they are called to be in some way its heart, revealing the true meaning of the organization of the earthly city. (n. 116)

Christians within Europe have a responsibility to work to build a body of legislation which is consonant with the moral law and where possible to correct morally defective laws. The first step on this path is to stress the Good News in the conviction that it is true and leads to freedom. The task is to challenge society anywhere with the message of Jesus Christ and the radical newness of his Gospel. A genuinely pluralistic system will not exclude religion from bringing its contribution to the public square nor will it unfairly exclude from the public square those who profess their religious convictions openly.

However, the Church has no mandate to attempt to generally impose on believers – much less on those who do not believe – specific political solutions. The Church can only propose what is derived from her Gospel mandate and the founded tradition of the Church. The Church must rather help enlighten consciences and provide support for Christian politicians and experts so that they can bring the newness of the Gospel message to the future of Europe in a way that is free from compromise and which will win the minds and hearts of others. The role of the Christian in Europe is not simply to ascertain sociologically what are the current value systems of European citizens, but to influence European public opinion, to evangelise it, i.e. to bring to the emerging European society, together with its Member States and component societies, that radical newness of the Gospel.

Christians can use only the instruments that are available and appropriate in this specific context, namely democratic means. They have, however, the right to full access to those means and to influence the process of discernment of what a future Europe of values, a Europe with a sense of purpose, a Europe of service in solidarity, should look like. I was very pleased that in recent meetings between the President of the European Commission, José Manuel Barroso, and Church leaders, Mr Barroso has expressed his desire to foster such a contribution by the Churches.

I conclude by once again quoting Pope John Paul II, who summarises the contribution of the Church to building a new Europe in the following terms:

> For her part, *in keeping with a healthy cooperation between the ecclesial community and political society, the Catholic Church is convinced that she can make a unique contribution* to the prospect of unification by offering the European institutions, in continuity with her tradition and in fidelity to the principles of her social teaching, the engagement of believing communities committed to bringing about the humanization of society on the basis of the Gospel, lived under the sign of hope. From this standpoint, the *presence of Christians,* properly trained and competent, is needed in the various European agencies and institutions, in order to contribute – with respect for the correct dynamics of democracy and through an exchange of proposals – to the shaping of a European social order which is increasingly respectful of every man and woman, and thus in accordance with the common good. (n. 117)

Notes

1. This paper was presented at the public meeting, *The Future of Europe: Challenges for Faith and Values*, held in Dublin on 26 September 2005.
2. Personal translation from the Italian: *Svolta per l'Europa: Chiesa e modernità nell'Europa dei rivolgimenti*, Edizioni Paoline, 1992. This is a translation of the collection of articles, *Wendezeit fuer Europa*, 1991.

References

Pope John Paul II (2003) *Ecclesia in Europa*, Post-Synodial Apostolic Exhortation, 28 June 2003.

Synod of Bishops (1991) *Final Declaration*, First Special Assembly for Europe, 13 December 1991.

Synod of Bishops (1999) *Final Message*, Second Special Assembly for Europe, 23 October 1999.

Fostering a Union of Permanent Contrasts

A Case for Turkish Membership of the European Union

Gillian Wylie

Introduction

After a long and convoluted story, which began in 1963, Turkey was finally admitted to the process of accessing membership of the European Union on 3 October 2005. In the teeth of very public opposition, led by Austria, there were doubts up to the last minute on that October night over whether admission to the process would occur. Despite this hard-won concession, the convulsions are not yet over. It is predicted that the process whereby Turkey will make further political, economic and legal preparations for joining the EU and then be assessed on the EU's criteria of readiness for accession – the Copenhagen Criteria – could take up to ten years. Yet even then there is the prospect of further convulsions to come. Although the EU developed the ostensibly objective Copenhagen Criteria in the 1990s for assessing the readiness for admission of the accession countries of eastern Europe, Turkey's eventual membership may be decided finally on highly subjective criteria. There is a sense already that European public opinion is against Turkish membership and with France's decision that it will hold a referendum at the point of Turkey's inclusion, the issue of how Turkey is perceived by publics and elites within the existing limits of the Union becomes crucial.[1]

Public negativity towards Turkey seems to be based on concerns, both economic and xenophobic, regarding migration, as well as a strong perception of cultural difference, rooted most obviously in Turkey's religious tradition. Such opinions among the general public have their mirrors at elite level in Europe. Austria may have made the most overt objections to Turkey's inclusion but its government is not alone in taking this stance. As well as having concerns about whether Turkey is 'too big and too poor' to join the Union without causing fundamental political and economic disruption, several influential figures in Europe have raised doubts about Turkey's historical, religious and cultural belonging to Europe. This is a view perhaps most bluntly put by the then Cardinal Ratzinger with his comment that Turkey has always been 'in permanent contrast to Europe' (*Le Figaro*, 2004).

The aim of this paper is to explore, and ultimately to reject, this idea that Turkey is Europe's 'permanent contrast'. There may well be geographical, historical and religious ambiguities about Turkey's Europeanness – ambiguities perceived by outsiders which indeed also rend Turkey internally – yet the argument of this paper will be that the idea of Europeanness is itself equally ambiguous. In the end, the construction of contemporary 'Europe' is a political and indeed ethical project. Understood from this perspective, there are compelling reasons favouring the inclusion of Turkey.

Turkey as Europe's 'Permanent Contrast'

Responding to the events of the night of 3 October 2005, the BBC website instigated a quiz testing general knowledge on Turkey.[2] One question asks: 'How much of Turkey is geographically in Europe?' The correct answer is given as 5 per cent. While the geographical limits of Europe, particularly to its east, have always been subjectively disputed, there is no doubt that this minuscule 5 per cent is just one of the reasons for the gamut of doubts cast over Turkey's 'Europeanness'.

The historical record concerning Turkey's relationship with Europe provides another lead into conflicting interpretations as to whether Turkey has been 'of Europe', or has been essentially Europe's defining 'other'.

To some, there is no room for historical doubt. Dominique Moisi (1999) has argued that: 'Turkey is not only Western, it is wholly European; Europe seems to have forgotten that Turkey has long been a key player in its history.' Substance for an assertion as strong as that can be found in a number of historical events. As the centre of the Ottoman Empire from the 1400s to the First World War, there is no doubt that the land now called Turkey has been involved in European history. Turkey's role as a key player included its long colonisation of large parts of south east Europe, as well as its involvement in European Concert of Power politics in the nineteenth century and its fateful participation on the losing side of the First World War, which left it dubbed by the Kaiser as 'the sick man of Europe' (note the telling *of* in that phrase).

Crucial though all of this was to the conduct of European politics, it does not mean that Turkey has been understood by all as belonging to Europe. That self-same history has been interpreted by others as revealing that Turkey has always been understood as a threat to Europe. According to Minou Reeves (2003): 'for five hundred years the Ottoman Turks ... represented Europe's most feared enemy.' Reeves points out that Turkey was perceived as posing not only a military but a religious and cultural threat (p. 101). The Muslim Ottoman Empire began with the sacking of Christian Constantinople. The military incursions of that Empire into Europe were understood not simply within the norms of 'balance of power' politics but as a threat to Christian civilisation itself. From this perspective, 'Europe' – both as physical place and as a civilisation – was saved twice when Turkish armies were stopped at the gates of Vienna, first in 1529 and again in 1683. It was saved on the second occasion by the Polish king, Jan Sobiewski, who saw the event as the clash of Christian Europe against the infidels (Davies, 1981, pp. 484–6). It is this interpretation of history that has allowed Norman Davis and others to suggest that the limits of Europe have been drawn by the clash with Islam – primarily as embodied by the Ottomans (Davies, 1996 and den Boer, 1995).

Beyond the end of the Ottoman Empire, the question of whether Turkey was of Europe or Europe's foil persisted throughout the twentieth century. In the chaos of the demise of the Ottoman Empire following the First World War, Greece (supported by western allies) waged war for territorial reasons on Turkey but was defeated by Ataturk's nationalist movement, which won independence for Turkey in 1923. Post-war Kemalist politics saw the emergence of a peculiar amalgam of 'authoritarian democracy' in Turkey, which entailed a complex mix of decreed westernisation (evidenced, for example, in secularism, parliamentary structures and some cultural practices), strongly hedged by the authoritarianism of the leader himself, an overbearing role for the military in political life, a weak judiciary and a nationalism which brooked no minority rights. From such politics emerged Turkey's well-known record of military suppression, torture and human rights abuse in relation to its Kurdish population (Pope and Pope, 1997, p. 59f.).

It seems that the fruits of these policies have given rise to an identity crisis that fragments Turkey to this day – and indeed makes its 'Europeanness' contentious from within, as well as from without. It is a secular state with an almost entirely Muslim population; a democracy with severe limitations (although now in a process of profound reforms); it has an urban elite that considers itself of the west aside an enormous rural, and often poor, population. All of this leaves nuanced outside observers struggling to compartmentalise Turkey. This is evident, for example, in the work of Nicole and Hugh Pope (1997), who opine that: 'Turkey defies easy categorisation – European, Western, Eastern, Islamic, fascist, anarchic – something of all, a category of its own.' (p. 2) Moreover, this eclectic identity is also recognised by many inside observers. Take, for instance, author Ohran Pamuk's novel, Snow, which brilliantly captures the uneasy mix of contemporary Turkish identities as the westernised main protagonist, a member of the Istanbul elite back from political exile in Germany, becomes trapped by blizzards in a god-forsaken eastern Turkish town. Here he becomes snowbound with a diverse cast of political Islamists, nationalists, ethnic separatists and secularists of all shades, whose differences are crystallised through their expressed attitudes of affiliation with or repugnance towards the west and Europe (Pamuk, 2004).

If the search for an answer as to whether contemporary Turkey is European concentrates only in such multifaceted historical legacies and current identity crises, it does become understandable why it is so difficult to offer a definitive response. Yet to look for the answer in the story of Turkey alone is to take an approach which assumes that while

Turkish identity is ambiguous, European identity and the idea of what constitutes Europe are not. As the next section will suggest, however, these are equally problematic assumptions.

Europe and the Permanency of Contrasts

As already noted, there is no consensus on the geographical limits of Europe. Imaginary lines have been drawn through the Ural Mountains, the Black Sea and the Aegean Sea in various attempts to demarcate Europe. But any such line remains inherently an act of imagination, more the result of socio-political than geographic reasoning[3] and thus dependent on the underlying subjective idea of what constitutes Europe for those drawing the lines. So, given its lack of physical or natural boundaries, 'Europe' is revealed to be a socially constructed idea. And given the propensity in European history for its peoples to assert perceived differences amongst themselves in violent ways, the question is inevitably begged as to what constitutes the commonalities that make the label 'Europe' applicable to a group of states. Mary Fulbrook (2001) finds her answer to this in the identification of common legacies which have shaped a peculiarly European political and cultural way. For Fulbrook, these include the imprints of Greek and Roman thought on political ideas and systems, the common hallmark of Christianity, the shared experience of being global colonisers, the philosophical and scientific legacies of the Enlightenment and the revolutionary experience which began in France in 1789 and which spawned the nationalist and socialist ideas which so affected Europe in the nineteenth and twentieth centuries (Fulbrook, 2001, pp. 274–6).

Any such attempt at holding together Europe's commonalities inevitably implies adopting amnesia about Europe's other histories. The equation of Europe with a homogenous Christian heritage glosses over the dividing lines driven through Europe by the marked divergences between eastern and western Christianity, never mind being utterly forgetful of the legacies of Islam in the history of Europe, particularly in Moorish Spain and in the Balkans, as well as of the impact of Jewish intellectual life and culture on the history of Europe.

The assumed shared experience of being colonisers neglects those, such as the Irish, who were colonised. The assumption that the Enlightenment provided a common experience to Europe is rendered problematic by the ways in which Enlightenment intellectuals of Europe's west disparaged its east as a somewhat barbaric 'demi-orient' (Woolf, 1994). And the tracing of Europe's political commonalities through the Greeks to the Enlightenment and on to revolutionary nationalism reads too much like a story of Europe as progress. It stops short of dwelling on the twentieth century's widespread experience of extremist nationalism, which cast certain Europeans as superior to others and, as a result, came close to destroying the continent.

If Europe's assumed historical commonalities do not really provide a basis for defining an unambiguous, shared, 'idea of Europe', this would seem to be a problem that has become ever more acute. It would appear ironic that the overriding commonality in Europe today is the intrinsically divisive idea of nationalism, with most citizens of the EU identifying themselves as national citizens first, and only in minimal numbers, and with vague definitions and little consequence, as Europeans next (Tsoukalis, 2003, p. 2; pp. 34–7).

Moreover, any assumed earlier homogeneity amongst Europeans, in terms of 'race', culture or religion, has been undone by the emergence since the Second World War of multicultural and religiously diverse societies throughout Europe. Arguably, there is no unambiguously identifiable, essential 'Europe'; rather, 'the idea of Europe remains elusive, susceptible to change and strongly conditioned by historical contingency' (Weaver, 1996, p. 205).

If we accept this reading of Europe as being ambiguous in identity and the outcome of changing social and historical imaginings, then on such grounds alone there can be little *prima facie* reason why equally ambiguous Turkey could not be considered to be of Europe. However, the argument for understanding Turkey as European can be put in a more constructive manner, by drawing attention to the grounds on which the most influential contemporary idea of Europe is being created.

Despite the violent histories, contrasting identities and contemporary diversity of Europeans, an idea of Europe as a politically and economically integrated entity has become institutionalised over the last fifty years. This entity, the European Union, now has such geographical reach, institutional complexity and political consequence that it has virtually colonised the idea and name of Europe (Tsoukalis, 2003, p. 4). Importantly, however, it is not an entity currently based on a widely shared identity (despite the ardent hopes of its founders and today's Europhiles) but on shared values, political structures and economic ties. In effect, the EU has defined contemporary Europeanness as being synonymous with democracy, human rights, the rule of law and the European social model and it has made these the measure of other countries' preparedness for inclusion in 'Europe'. As Turkey engages in the reforms necessary for it to meet these criteria, it becomes unambiguously European in this contemporary sense.

The European Union as a Community of Values

The European Union has become the most solid political project to date aimed at the creation of an integrated Europe. Again, it is worth noting there have been several such projects, of varying degrees of concreteness, and each embodying a different concept of Europe. Only a decade separated the influence of Count Richard Coudenhove-Kalergi's pacific Pan-Europa movement of the 1920s from the Nazi's attempt to unite Europe belligerently under an order based on racial hierarchy (Delanty, 1995, pp. 107–8; Pagden, 2002, p. 7).

The project for European integration which emerged following that horrendous experience was based on the idea that integration would be best fostered pragmatically. Through the forging of economic ties in the first instance, integration would 'spill-over' into other areas, especially the political life of Member States. Underpinning all this practical activity, however, were a set of values to be realised, identified by Weiler (1999) as being peace, prosperity and supra-nationalism (p. 259). Membership of this community of values was offered to all European states as a right in the 1957 Treaty of Rome, but it was the inherent ambiguity of knowing who is 'European', as discussed above, which prompted clarification of this in a 1978 European Council decision. According to this decision, Europeanness entailed 'a constitutional guarantee of democratic principles and human rights' (Borzel and Risse, 2004). Further clarification of the essentially political and ethical bases for being judged to be 'European' have come in various treaties since then, including the Maastricht Treaty (which reiterated the 1978 decision) and in the currently parked Constitutional Treaty with its inclusion of the Charter of Fundamental Rights. It is worth noting also in relation to Turkish accession that the fraught discussion around whether the Constitutional Treaty should include reference to God and Europe's Christian heritage ultimately both underlined the secularism of the EU as an entity and revealed the multiplicity of Europe's religious heritages, Christian and other (*The Christian Century*, 2003). In addition to these Treaty-based definitions of Europeanness, the Copenhagen Criteria stipulated that a country was judged to be ready for accession to the EU on the basis of possessing a functioning democracy, the rule of law, respect for minority rights, a market economy and the ability to adopt the *acquis communautaire* into national law. All of this implies that 'Europe', as now understood and constructed within the European Union, is a political–ethical project and not an essential identity.

For several years, Turkey has been making progress towards realising the Copenhagen Criteria. The 'golden carrot' of membership has been taking ever-increasing effect in Turkey, with successive governments implementing policies designed to meet the conditions. Thus, the state has lifted the ban on broadcasting in Kurdish, released some Kurdish activists from jail, abolished the death penalty, adopted a zero tolerance policy towards the use of torture and taken measures to curtail the influence of the military in politics (Hughes, 2004; Dorronsoro, 2003). Moreover, the Turkish state has engaged seriously with efforts to create peace in Cyprus. Undeniably, these reforms have caused serious political tensions inside Turkey. The country is sometimes still caught between western liberalism and its more authoritarian traditions, as illustrated by events such as the national row over the proposed criminalisation of adultery[4] or the criminal charges brought against Pamuk for having written about the Armenian Genocide. Much reform has yet to be implemented. Yet, there is little doubt amongst observers that Turkey's polity has been revolutionised by the process of EU accession. By implication, if the EU were to reject Turkey after all this change, and yet more reform to come, it would de-legitimise itself and its claim to be a community of values (Diez and Rumelili, 2004, pp. 33–5).

Conclusion

The argument of this paper is based on the premise that Europe is not a determinate place with a singular identity. Rather, like Turkish identity, Europeanness involves the coexistence of numerous permanently contrasting identities. What does exist as the most solid expression of the idea of Europe today is dependent not on common heritage, religious foundation, or shared contemporary identity, but on a political project aimed at constructing European integration, based on certain foundational values and the fostering of the political arrangements necessary to realise them. Turkey's revolutionary reform process makes it eminently European in this sense of the word. Moreover, Turkey's inclusion in the Union would do much to ensure the further realisation of the foundational values behind this European project. In particular, the desire to foster peace would be enhanced by the inclusion of a majority Muslim state in apparently 'Christian' Europe. Such an act would signal the undoing of the inevitability of the 'clash of civilisations' by creating a Europe which demonstrated the possibilities of living peaceably despite the permanency of contrasting identities.

Notes

1. A Eurobarometer survey of public opinion, carried out in May–June 2005, revealed that 52 per cent of interviewees across the EU were opposed to Turkish accession (Eurobarometer, 2005).

2. BBC News (2005) 'Take the Turkey Test!'. (http://news.bbc.co.uk/1/hi/world/europe/4305656.stm)
3. See, for example, 'Transcontinental Nation', from Wikipedia, the free encyclopedia. (http://en.wikipedia.org/wiki/ Transcontinental_nation)
4. See, for example, Jonny Dymond, 'Analysis: Turkey, Adultery and the EU', BBC. (http://news.bbc.co.uk/2/hi/europe/3659298.stm)

References

Borzel, Tanja A. and Thomas Risse (2004) 'One Size Fits All! EU Policies for the Promotion of Human Rights, Democracy and the Rule of Law', Paper presented at workshop, *Promoting Democracy and the Rule of Law: EU and US Strategies and Instruments*, Center on Democracy, Development, and the Rule of Law (CDDRL), Stanford Institute for International Studies (SIIS), Stanford University, 4–5 October 2004. (www.cddrl.stanford/edu)

Davies, Norman (1984) *God's Playground: A History of Poland, Volume 1 – The Origins to 1795*, Oxford: Oxford University Press.

Davies, Norman (1996) *Europe: A History*, Oxford: Oxford University Press.

Delanty, Gerard (1995) *Inventing Europe: Idea, Identity, Reality*, London: Macmillan.

den Boer, Pim (1995) 'Europe to 1914: The Making of an Idea' in Kevin Wilson and Jan van der Dussen (eds) *The History of the Idea of Europe*, revised edition, Milton Keynes: Open University Press.

Diez, Thomas and Bahar Rumelili (2004) 'Open the Door: Turkey and the European Union', *The World Today*, August–September 2004, pp. 33–5.

Dorronsoro, Gilles (2003) 'The EU and Turkey: Between Geopolitics and Social Engineering' in Roland Dannreuther (ed.) *European Union Foreign and Security Policy: Towards a Neighbourhood Strategy*, London: Routledge.

Eurobarometer (2005) *Eurobarometer 63: Public Opinion in the European Union* (fieldwork May–June 2005; publication July 2005). (http://europa.eu.int/comm/public_opinion/archives/eb/eb63/eb63.4_en_first.pdf)

Fulbrook, Mary (ed.) (2001) *Europe Since 1945*, Oxford: Oxford University Press (Short Oxford History of Europe Series).

Hughes, Kirsty (2004) *Turkey and the EU: Just Another Enlargement?: Exploring the Implications of Turkish Accession*, Brussels: Friends of Europe. (www.friendsofeurope.org)

Le Figaro, 'Cardinal Ratzinger: Identifier la Turquie a l'Europe Serait une Erreu', 13 August 2004.

Moisi, Dominique (1999) 'Dreaming of Europe', *Foreign Policy*, No. 115, Summer 1999, pp. 44–59.

Pagden, Anthony (ed.) (2002) *The Idea of Europe: From Antiquity to the European Union*, Cambridge: Cambridge University Press.

Pamuk, Orhan (2004) *Snow*, London: Faber and Faber.

Pope, Nicole and Hugh Pope (1997) *Turkey Unveiled: A History of Modern Turkey*, London: John Murray.

Reeves, Minou (2003) *Muhammed in Europe – 1000 Years of Western Myth-Making*, New York: New York University Press.

The Christian Century, 'Unholy Row on God's Place in EU Constitution', 5 April 2003. (www.findarticles.com/p/articles/ mi_m1058/is_7_120/ai_ 99988479)

Tsoukalis, Loukas (2003) *What Kind of Europe?* Oxford: Oxford University Press.

Waever, Ole (1996) 'Europe Since 1945: Crisis to Renewal' in Kevin Wilson and Jan van der Dussen (eds) *What is Europe? The History of the Idea of Europe*, revised edition, Milton Keynes: Open University Press.

Weiler, J.H.H. (1999) *The Constitution of Europe: 'Do the New Clothes have an Emperor?' and other Essays on European Integration*, Cambridge: Cambridge University Press.

Wolff, Larry (1994) *Inventing Eastern Europe: The Map of Civilization on the Mind of the Enlightenment*, Stanford: Stanford University Press.

Europe and the Roman Catholic Church

Gerry O'Hanlon SJ

The political mood in Europe at time of writing is rather querulous. The proposed Constitutional Treaty has been rejected by referenda in France and The Netherlands. There is tetchiness over budgetary matters (including different approaches to reform of the Common Agricultural Policy and to allocation of funds to accession states) and there remains a distinct cooling of attitude on the part of some to Turkish accession. Because of fears about terrorism, there is a tendency to get tougher on immigration control as well as a new uncertainty about integration policies in Member States such as France and the United Kingdom. Real differences are apparent on how a social model of Europe can be balanced with the workings of the free market. And all the time there is the impression that ordinary citizens find it difficult to engage with European issues, so that the 'democratic deficit' is in danger of leading to the kind of self-interested and isolated nationalism which the founders of the European Communities sought to combat and which is all the more out of place in our increasingly globalised world.

One gets the sense of the need for a new vision and for a shared commitment to that vision. *The Tablet* (26 November 2005) reported that: 'Catholic Bishops meeting in Brussels have welcomed the European Commission's renewed efforts to bring Europe closer to its citizens through a more coherent communications strategy.' (p. 33) Bishop Josef Homeyer, President of the Commission of the Bishops' Conferences of the European Community (COMECE), is quoted as saying: 'People are very insecure at the moment. The EU is faced with a very serious situation – perhaps the most serious since it came into being 50 years ago … yes, we are in a deep crisis … But this is an opportunity to relaunch Europe.' And, in this context, he signaled the willingness of COMECE and the Roman Catholic Church to make a positive contribution.

It might seem surprising to many that the Catholic Church sees itself in a position to make a positive contribution to a re-launch of the European project. What resources does the Church bring to this re-launch and how credible is its contribution likely to be?

The Roman Catholic Contribution

Churches have an important role to play in European civil society and do so in many ways – through schools, universities, hospitals, publications and so on. I want to focus on one, albeit central, aspect of the Catholic Church's contribution, namely its teaching on Europe. The most authoritative contemporary document articulating this teaching is the Apostolic Exhortation, *Ecclesia in Europa,* of the late Pope John Paul II (2003), which followed on from the Synod of Bishops' Second Special Assembly for Europe in 1999. The members of the Church itself are the primary target audience for the document, but its content has relevance to a wider public.

What comes through in this document is Pope John Paul's understanding that Europe is going through a difficult time of fear and his desire to offer it hope for the future. He does so because he clearly values the European project, seeing in it an 'affirmation of the transcendent dignity of the human person, the value of reason, freedom, democracy, the constitutional state and the distinction between political life and religion' (n. 109). He notes positively the adherence to values of solidarity and subsidiarity in the European Union (n. 110), so that at least normatively it wants to include the poor and less strong and respect national and cultural differences. He does so, too, because he is conscious of the responsibility and great potential Europe has for the rest of our world: 'Saying "Europe" must be equivalent to saying "openness"'. (n. 111) This means openness not just to immigrants but also to the rest of our increasingly globalised world so that we need to rethink 'international cooperation in terms of a new culture of solidarity' (n. 111). To this end, he encourages the different European institutions to continue to develop in ways that can better promote values such as solidarity, justice and peace in our world.

Much of this could, of course, be written by a non-religious person, as the late Pope implicitly acknowledges when he states that the solid foundations needed for the building up of the new Europe are those authentic values grounded in the universal moral law written on the heart of every man and woman. He quotes from his letter of October 2000 to Cardinal Miloslav Vlk, President of the Council of European Episcopal Conferences: 'Not only can Christians join with all people of good will in working to build up this great project, but they are also called to be in some way its heart, revealing the true meaning of the organisation of the earthly city' (n. 116). There need not be any triumphalism involved in this specification of the Christian role: Pope John Paul does not want a return to the confessional state (n. 117), only a respectful dialogue between the European Union and religious confessions which can be to mutual advantage (n. 114). And if Europe itself must learn from its failures to handle conflict well, from its history especially in the last century 'of totalitarian ideologies and extreme forms of nationalism' (n. 112), then the Church, too, must be careful not to be seen as a factor of division and discord: 'Would this not be one of the greatest scandals of our time?'(n. 119)

However, John Paul does, of course, want to say that Christianity has specific resources to contribute to this project which will be realised together with all men and women of good will. He is certainly referring here to various international, European and national institutions through which the Roman Catholic Church acts in our world (n. 116–19 especially). But more particularly he is referring to Jesus Christ and the Gospel itself, with the Good News that we need not be afraid, that our grounds for hope are sure, and that values such as freedom, justice, peace and forgiveness as found in the Christian tradition (not least in Catholic social teaching) can be a powerful reinforcement of humanitarian efforts towards a better world. And so, 'in keeping with a healthy cooperation between the ecclesial community and political society, the Catholic Church is convinced that she can make a unique contribution ... by offering the European institutions, in continuity with her tradition and in fidelity to the principles of her social teaching, the engagement of believing communities committed to bringing about the humanisation of society on the basis of the Gospel, lived under the sign of hope.' (n. 117) From the Gospel then can come a new enthusiasm for Europe (n. 120).

The Pope, therefore, is offering the Church's support for those humanitarian values consonant with the Gospel, which can form the basis for a vision of Europe into the future. He goes further, of course, in diagnosing the current fear and lack of energy in relation to the European project as due to the loss of its spiritual roots, and in prescribing a new evangelisation of Europe as being the way to reinvigorate the project: *'Do not be afraid! The Gospel is not against you, but for you.* This is confirmed by the fact that Christian inspiration is capable of transforming political, cultural and economic groupings into a form of coexistence in which all Europeans will feel at home and will form a family of nations from which other areas of the world can draw fruitful inspiration.' (n. 121)

Value of this Contribution

Ecclesia in Europa threads a fine line between allowing for the rightful autonomy of earthly affairs, as articulated in *Gaudium et Spes* (Vatican II, 1965, n. 36), and yet refusing to countenance any dualism between the Gospel and public life. It does so well: the separation of Church and State is clear, while the potential for constructive dialogue is also asserted.

For Christians the content is helpful, and even inspiring. This is a wake-up call to rouse us from apathy about the European project, to appreciate its great potential to realise important Gospel values, not least the peace that has come to the original EU members through the workings-out of the Franco–German alliance and the freedom and justice, long over-due, which are characteristic of the new accession states of eastern Europe. It remains to be seen whether the more cautious tone of the document concerning Islam might not change as the injunction to grow in knowledge of other religions is realised (n. 57) – and certainly this remains a key task for the Churches, not least in the context of talks leading up to the possibility of Turkish accession to the EU.

But there is also an opportunity here for secular humanitarians from the liberal and social traditions to respond positively. For many secularists, religion can be almost synonymous with superstition or divisiveness or indeed both. And so there can be a tendency among liberals to be less than tolerant – in fact illiberal – towards the religious viewpoint, be it fundamentalist or more mainstream. Many are now questioning the wisdom of this stance. They are doing so, firstly, because, stubbornly, religion has not and will not go away: it remains a potent force in many people's lives, and so politically it is important to try to understand it. And if at its worst (the religious wars in Europe of the past, the appeal to Islam in support of terror in the present and the misuse of the Gospel by the 'religious right' in the USA in response) this potent force is destructive, then at its best it is liberating: the influence of religious factors, starting in Poland, on the fall of communism was considerable. In either case, it needs to be understood, not dismissed or denied. Secondly, and more significantly, post-modernism has trenchantly criticised what it diagnoses as the bias of modernity's rejection of the transcendent and is calling for a re-enchantment of our world. In this context, the poignant words of Nietzsche are apt: 'Where has God gone? ... I will tell you. We have slain him – you and I ... but how did we do it? How could we drink up the sea? Who gave us the sponge to wipe out the whole horizon? What did we do when we unchained the earth from its sun?... Do we not now wander through an endless nothingness? Does empty space not breath upon us? Is it not colder now? Is not night coming, and even more night? Must we not light lanterns at noon? God is dead. God stays dead. And we have slain him ...' (Quoted in Thornhill, 2000, pp. 31–2)

If this existential loneliness and sense of demoralising aimlessness can be assuaged by a divine presence that is not simply wish-fulfilment but, rather, is true, then surely our situation is so much better? And if this is a step too far, too quickly, then at least it surely makes sense for religious and secularists to come to some kind of respectful settlement of their dispute so that together they can get on with their common aim of striving for a better Europe and a better world? Cannot religion be a help in replenishing the moral capital of liberalism, be it in its modern or postmodern form and without threat to the gains of the enlightenment? (Vallely, 2005)

Credibility of the Church's Contribution

The content of a teaching may propose what is true and good and yet for different reasons, not least the credibility of its source, it may not be heard. It seems that many people, including those who might describe themselves as being on the edges of the Roman Catholic Church, no longer listen sympathetically or at all to what the Church officially teaches. What can the Church do to enhance its credibility?

The late Pope himself has some ideas on this topic. He notes the need for conversion within the Church itself: 'One sees how *our ecclesial communities* are struggling with weaknesses, weariness and divisions. They too need to hear the voice of the Bridegroom, who invites them to conversion ... In this way *Jesus Christ is calling our Churches in Europe to conversion ...*' (n. 23) This need for conversion, for a lived, intimate contact with Jesus Christ will, of course, be central to the 'new evangelization' which John Paul II called for so insistently. It is what distinguishes the Church from being just any other well-meaning NGO. The Pope's own transparent faith was exemplary in this respect. We as Church in Europe need to pray for this conversion and to appreciate its centrality for our mission. Holiness has a certain transparency, which carries its own conviction even to non-believers.

But holiness – which is what conversion is about – is one among several factors which are likely to impact on Church credibility. As well as the centrality of the spiritual in the lives of human beings, several other dimensions spring to mind as being so important as to affect the credibility of any institution which claims to teach about what it is that makes up a good and happy life. I refer in particular here to the dimensions of money, sex and power. With regard to the economic dimension, while there are negative comments sometimes about the wealth of the Church, it seems to me that its teaching on wealth is well-respected and the witness of many individual Christians reinforces this teaching in a way that prevents this becoming a major stumbling block to credibility. It is different with respect to sex and power, however, so that I wish now to focus more particularly on these two important dimensions of human living.

The Church and Sex

For most human beings the search for meaning in life – and so for God – is most real in the struggles and joys surrounding the attempt to relate to and love significant others – parents, siblings, spouses, children, and so on. Because this is so, for Catholics the credibility of the Church will depend significantly on the extent to which they can expect wise counsel with respect to this central aspect of life. The richness of Church teaching concerning the fundamental principles that should inform such key relationships – respect, commitment, fidelity, love, for example – is overshadowed by the fact that many Catholics are disappointed, not to say dismayed, with what the Church has to say with regard to aspects of sexuality. This inevitably leads to a lack of confidence in Church teaching generally.

What is at issue here? In conversation with committed Catholics over the years many points have been put to me on this matter. Let the eponymous Deirdre act as spokesperson for these views. Deirdre is in her thirties, believes in God, has been baptised a Catholic, has studied some theology and 'hangs in' with the Church even though she disagrees with important aspects of Church teaching in the sexual area. She respects greatly the Church's wisdom in locating the powerful drive of sexuality within a more integral emotional and personal context, and within the parameters of a relationship of exclusive commitment. She appreciates also the condemnation of the exploitation of women in Church teaching, and agrees with the cautions against the development of a 'contraceptive mentality'.

Nonetheless, Deirdre cannot understand or accept the normative weight and value given to the distinction between natural and artificial methods of birth control. It seems to her that this distinction relies on an excessively physicalist interpretation of natural law, which is not applied with the same absoluteness to other areas of life – for example, to the use of medication or to the judgements to be made about genetically modified food. She knows that the Church has only relatively recently accorded equal value to the notion that sex is important for the good of the relationship of a married couple (the unitive dimension) as well as for purposes of fertility (the procreative dimension), and she is concerned that there remains apparent in the Church an excessively fearful and controlling attitude to sexuality in general and to women in particular. She wonders if this attitude is not due, in part at least, to the fact that the teaching authority of her Church is still very much in the hands of male celibates.

And this doubt about the reliability of Church teaching in the area of contraception – which she is aware is widely shared by many other Catholics and, indeed, by many theologians – leads her to question the wisdom of teaching in related areas. She appreciates the value of Church teaching on abstinence in the context of the fight against HIV / AIDS, but is aghast that there is not a more open acceptance of the morality of condom use in the context of disease prevention. She has some friends who are divorced and are now in stable second unions but are not welcome to participate fully in the Eucharist. She wonders in this context if the Church has not over-emphasised its theology of Eucharist as a *sign* of unity over the other tradition of Eucharist as a *means* to unity – a tradition which, she understands, is normative in the Orthodox Churches and which Rome has never seen as a stumbling block to unity with these Churches. She thinks it is odd that these friends of hers are made to feel less comfortable joining the line of people going up to receive communion than people who have been involved in corporate greed, racism and tax evasion.

Deirdre wonders if the designation of homosexuality as 'objective disorder' is again not due to a one-sided interpretation of the natural law, as well as being a nightmare in terms of communicating a message of respect for people who are homosexual. She values the gift that celibacy is for the Church and is aware that a married clergy is not without its own problems, but wonders nevertheless if the discipline of the western Church concerning compulsory clerical celibacy is desirable or indeed sustainable, given the needs of the Church and the drop in priestly vocations, not to mention the good in itself of having clergy who are married.

She is incredulous and angry at the Church's refusal to consider the ordination of women and at its attempt to stifle discussion on the topic. She is aware that already in the 1970s the Pontifical Biblical Commission had stated that there is no absolute ban on women priests from a scriptural point of view. While acknowledging that there is a long tradition of priesthood being reserved to males, she knows that other venerable traditions of the Church have changed over time, often due to shifts in cultural and moral sensibility (for example, the teaching on slavery), so the length of the tradition is not in itself an insurmountable obstacle to change. And if the argument for the status quo is to be sought in a theological anthropology, which asserts that male and females are equal but different in a complementary way, suggesting the suitability of priesthood for men and not women, then Deirdre begs to demur. She knows that this anthropology is controverted and is not convinced by it.

Even allowing for the notion that the equality between women and men does contain within it a difference between male and female that is not simply biological, Deirdre, relying on her own experience but aware too of the body of academic work which supports her view, would want to interpret this difference less rigidly. She affirms that women too are made in the image and likeness of God, women too can exercise leadership roles, and only a very paradoxically literalist understanding of symbolism would deny that women too can represent Jesus Christ in his love for us unto death. If scripture, tradition and theology can offer no conclusive obstacle to the ordination of women, she finds it unacceptable that the Church wants to curtail further discussion of this matter. All these issues coming together create a doubt for Deirdre about the reliability of Church teaching in the contested and highly significant field of bio-ethics in general.

Apart altogether from the particular answers to any one of these difficult and extremely relevant questions, Deirdre senses what she can only describe as a controlling approach and a reliance on a particular form of natural law and anthropological essentialism which result in a stance that lacks compassion and even wisdom. So, for example, because the physical act of intercourse can, and sometimes gladly does, lead to conception does not mean, in her view, that it should always, even in principle, do so. The meaning of that physical act has to be understood, in her view, in a wider context, which takes account of many factors other than the physical alone. And similarly, as already indicated, she is not convinced that, given all we know nowadays about gender and about the new roles which women have assumed, maleness and femaleness should be differentiated in such an absolute way as to indicate so clearly that God cannot call women to ordination in the Church.

Deirdre knows that in expressing these disagreements and doubts she will be understood by some as taking the easy way out, unable to accept the 'hard sayings' of the Gospel, asking the Church to accommodate revealed truth to modern and post-modern culture in a reductive way. But she rejects this understanding. She says simply that she believes the Church is wrong on some of these issues, may be wrong on others, and has changed many times in the past. She argues that 'hardness' and 'softness' are not properly criteria of truth and so do not come into the question — she adheres to the wonderful Good News of Jesus Christ about love of friend and enemy. This Good News brings its own suffering and joy and is at the centre of the bigger picture which, she believes, is too often obscured by excessive attention to and insistence on relatively insignificant details of sexuality which somehow seem almost divorced from the wider context of love in which they belong.

In fact, Deirdre is only too well aware that our overly-sexualised culture is all at sea and that the Church has some wonderfully wise and helpful things to say in this area, but she believes that because its stance on particular issues is so mistaken then it loses much of its credibility. She herself now listens to the latest Church pronouncements on sexuality with something of a sigh and half an ear, and this has begun to affect her respect for the authority of the Church in other areas too.

Deirdre's position, then, does bring up the related issue of power and authority, to which we now turn. Her hermeneutic of mistrust in the sexual area has been reinforced by the revelations concerning clerical sexual abuse of minors and in particular by the inadequate response of Church authorities.

The Church and Power

In *Ecclesia in Europa*, Pope John Paul II recognises that the credible proclamation of the Gospel to Europe depends, among other things, on the service of theologians who are encouraged to 'persevere in the service which they render, to combine their scholarly research with prayer, to engage in attentive dialogue with contemporary culture, to adhere faithfully to the Magisterium and to cooperate with it in a spirit of communion in truth and charity, immersed in the *sensus fidei* of the People of God and helping to nurture it.' (n. 52) It is wise that the theologian pays attention to these several sources – and there are others too – of theological truth rather than playing a solo game. It is wise in particular that theologians have a real desire to think with the Church, to have a positive attitude towards the acceptance of Church teaching, without, of course, suspending all critical faculties.

However, a difficulty arises when there is a conflict between the different sources of theological truth. Such a conflict clearly arises in the sexual area, in particular with the teaching in the encyclical, *Humanae Vitae* (Pope Paul VI, 1968). The eponymous Deirdre is not an isolated figure: there is 'the virtual non-reception by many theologians and a large percentage of the laity in some countries of *Humanae Vitae* on contraception' (O'Donnell, 1996, p. 401). Of course it is true that the 'sense of faith' of the faithful and their reception of truth – both significant technical terms within theology – are not a simple matter of counting heads, nor are they a precondition of true magisterial teaching. However, reception – the acceptance by the faithful that what their pastors teach is authentic and life-giving – is an important sign that teaching is definitive. Where there is non-reception, serious questions must be asked, even if it is not always immediately clear what the reasons might be.

These reasons might have to do with human perversity, blindness, hardness of heart on the part of the receiving faithful, but they might also have to do with a teaching that is false in whole or in part, and so cannot be binding (O'Donnell, 1996, p. 401).

Perhaps the task of a bishop was never easy, but certainly it is true that few people in Ireland today would envy those who have been called to serve the Gospel in this way. How might bishops, many of whom would claim no special theological expertise, respond to someone like Deirdre? I think the issue here is not so much one of theological expertise *per se*, but rather a decision to listen carefully to what people are saying, to try to sift and discern what is genuine and true from what may be more superficial, and then to bring this to the table of the Episcopal Conference and higher. Of course, that decision – to listen, discern, represent – does imply a theology of what it is to be a bishop that may be somewhat different from the prevailing one. Many bishops seem to feel that Rome leaves them very little freedom in these matters of Church teaching, but the theology of episcopal collegiality in Vatican II surely implies that a bishop has a duty to listen to the Spirit in his own life and in his own diocese. It is only by doing this that collegiality and a sense of what all the faithful think and believe can have any real meaning. Otherwise, collegiality simply becomes another name for a rubber-stamping conformity and the Church is robbed of the richness that comes from diversity, a diversity that can include doctrinal development.

It is often said, when discussion of these topics comes up, that the Church is not a democracy, as if this was the answer to all issues about power and truth. In fact, there have always been democratic aspects to the Gospel and the Church, at least as understood in the wider sense that is sufficient for my proposal here. What I mean by this is that neither did Jesus Christ rely solely on himself to come to truth, and nor has the Church done so down through the centuries. We can be sure that Jesus learned from and was corrected by his parents, his community and others. It seems that he learned something very significant about his mission – that it might extend beyond the Jewish people – from his encounter with the SyroPhoenician woman (Mk 7:24–30). Peter

EUROPE AND THE ROMAN CATHOLIC CHURCH

certainly learned from Paul – and indeed from his own dreams! – about the mission to the Gentiles. The bishops of the fourth century learned from the laity what the Council of Nicea was asserting about the truth of who Jesus Christ is. Galileo has taught the Church, even if he was not heard at the time. John Courtney Murray influenced the Church to change a centuries-old stance on religious freedom and was only one of many at the Second Vatican Council whose positions were vindicated in a way that resulted in significant doctrinal development against what seemed to many like unchangeable Church teaching.

Ecclesiastical historian Eamon Duffy has written extensively and well about the wonderful gift to the Roman Catholic Church that is present in the Magisterium and especially in the Papal teaching office (Duffy, 2004, chapters 7–9, 16–19). They are essential to hold the diversity of the Church together in a communion that allows the designation 'universal' to be applied. Many other Christian traditions, with all their strengths, have a propensity to fragmentation that makes them look with admiration to what we as Catholics enjoy. But if we should treasure this gift we should also seek to enjoy it in a way which avoids a certain tendency to claim that all teaching is equally definitive and also integrates other values, not least respect for truth and that careful listening to the faithful which I have spoken about and which bishops have a special opportunity to foster, as well as a more generous and accountable attitude and procedure in monitoring theological reflection.

One of the lessons we have all learned from the terrible scandal of child sexual abuse by priests and religious is surely that silence and denial about important truths are not good ways to proceed. In the matter of child sexual abuse, they have led to the unspeakable suffering of victims as well as to a strong anger, a sense of betrayal and almost even despair among so many others in the Church. But in other areas also, including those referred to in this article, silence and denial at best bring a false peace, without sure foundations. At worst, they encourage an anti-intellectualism and mediocrity of mind and heart which shirk awkward questions and answers and which run the risk of laying intolerable burdens on the shoulders of good men and women.

Pope John Paul II has quite rightly condemned the 'totalitarian ideologies' (n. 112) which darkened Europe in the twentieth century: we as Church need to avoid any totalitarian tendencies in our own conduct of affairs, combining firmness of decision with a serene confidence in the power of the Holy Spirit to bring truth and life out of open debate and even disagreement. It is surely not healthy to live as a Church with disagreements that can only be aired at the cost of being labelled disloyal?

Conclusion

I have indicated that Church teaching on Europe has an extremely important and valuable contribution to make, not least at the visionary level but also in critiquing wrong turns and lending additional moral weight to directions that are good. I have also pointed out that there is a danger that the Church's voice will not be heard as widely as it deserves – both within and outside its own community – for reasons that are not directly associated with the content of its teaching on Europe. I refer to the credibility problem that the Church as institution has – in particular, with its teaching in the sexual area and its tendency to exercise power in a way which stifles dialogue with opposing voices. This credibility problem extends, of course, to non-Catholics as well as Catholics: references to the universal moral law and natural law do not convince non-Catholics when they issue in the kind of sexual teaching that I have referred to and when they are commended to the assent of the faithful by what are perceived as excessive reliance on appeals to the power of authority in contrast to judgements emerging from a more reasoned and inclusive dialogue in search of the truth.

There are signs of hope that this situation may change. Many bishops now encourage more lay involvement in Church affairs, not least by the establishment of parish councils. Lay people themselves are more theologically literate and pastorally competent, and many want to claim their baptismal mission by playing a more active role in the Church. Some bishops have shown a willingness to listen carefully to what people are saying, to face the awkward questions, to show a collegial independence of mind in the answers they give and to bring their concern to higher bodies in ways that are encouraging. And Pope Benedict XVI (2005) in his beautiful encyclical letter, *Deus Caritas Est*, has shown that when the Church speaks out wisely in matters of love and sex, fair-minded people are appreciative. However, there is still a long way to go; resistance is deep and a big cultural shift is required.

There is an 'elephant in the room' of the Catholic polity. It is its teaching on certain aspects of sexuality and related areas, and its exercise of power in seeking to impose this teaching. There is a delicate discernment to be made – are Catholics who disagree with this teaching more in tune with the 'signs of the times' or are they simply disobedient, perhaps selfish, selling out to the prevailing values of the culture? And given that many do agree with the teaching and have made considerable sacrifices to follow it, given that despite its more general unpopularity in this important area of human living, the Church does still retain a great deal of credibility in other areas, perhaps it is better to go on ignoring the elephant rather than putting the Church through the turmoil of a review of teaching with all the likely concomitant turmoil and conflict?

But there was turmoil in the early Church when the mission to the Gentiles was being discussed, and many times later when significant changes happened. Surely we need to be more confident, if not in ourselves, then in the power of God's spirit to lead us into the deep and into truth? I am arguing that the non-reception of Church teaching in a central aspect of people's lives damages the credibility of the Church and that it would be a good thing to examine the reasons for this non-reception and emerge from the uneasy silence which now obtains. Cardinal Martini has several times called for a new Council of the Church, in the context of discussing some of the issues I have referred to. And in Ireland there have been intermittent calls for a Synod or some such gathering. I believe these kind of fora, organised with good consultation and participation, may well be what is needed at this time to release the imagination and renew the energy of our Church so as to allow the Good News of Jesus Christ be heard more clearly.

References

Duffy, Eamon (2004) *Faith of our Fathers: Reflections on Catholic Tradition*, New York and London: Continuum.

O'Donnell, Christopher, O.Carm (1996) *Ecclesia, A Theological Encyclopedia of the Church*, Collegeville, Minnesota: The Liturgical Press.

Pope Benedict XI (2005) *Deus Caritas Est (God is Love)*, Encyclical Letter, 25 December 2005, London: Catholic Truth Society.

Pope John Paul II (2003) *Ecclesia in Europa (The Church in Europe)*, Post-Synodial Apostolic Exhortation, 28 June 2003.

Pope Paul VI (1968) *Humanae Vitae (Human Life)* Encyclical Letter, 25 July 1968, London: Catholic Truth Society.

Thornhill, John (2000) *Modernity: Christianity's Estranged Child Reconstructed*, Grand Rapids, Michigan: Eerdmans.

Vallely, Paul (2005) 'What Europe Now Needs is Faith', *The Tablet*, 12 November 2005, pp. 6–7.

Vatican II (1965) *Gaudium et Spes* (Pastoral Constitution on the Church in the Modern World), 7 December 1965 in Austin Flannery OP (ed.) *Vatican II: The Conciliar and Post Conciliar Documents*, revised edition, Dublin: Dominican Publications, 1988.

The Future of the European Union

Economic Growth, Social Cohesion and Sustainability[1]
David Begg

According to his biographer, François Ducêne, Jean Monnet had a clear vision of Europe as a political entity shaping the course of world events. Ducêne cites an extract from a handwritten letter sent by Monnet to the French Prime Minister on 23 August 1950:

> Of all the countries of the West, the United States is the readiest to accept change and listen to long straight talk, so long as one throws a constructive idea into the ring. The United States are not imperialist, they are efficient ... Alone, they will not develop the political vision of which the world stands in need. I think that is our task. (Ducêne, 1994)

The last sentence seems almost prophetic. If the earlier part of the paragraph is more generous than current circumstances will allow, then let it be remembered that Monnet was an Atlanticist, speaking of an America that favoured European integration. It was a polity much removed from the antipathy of Donald Rumsfeld, US Secretary of Defense, to 'Old Europe'.

More than fifty years on, the mission of the European Union is no longer to prevent wars of the type that disfigured the twentieth century, but rather to be an alternative pole of western influence – alternative to the United States, that is. The hope of those who want an integrated, political entity is that it can tame the worst excesses of globalisation by presenting to the world the social market model as against the more brutal turbo capitalism which is the hallmark of the United States.

It is true, of course, that not everyone takes this view. The alternative holds that the social market model is an outdated failure, straining under the burden of unaffordable welfare entitlements and employment rights. A serious dose of liberal market economics is needed to enable it to compete with the more virile American business model. This debate has come to the fore as a result of the rejection of the European Constitutional Treaty by France in May 2005, but not in the way the 'No' voters had expected.

Tony Blair seized on the unfolding crisis, and the happy coincidence of Britain's EU Presidency, to push for more market liberalisation, despite the fact that this vision is precisely what the French people thought they were voting against.

When it was promulgated following the March 2000 meeting of the Council of Ministers, the Lisbon Strategy sought to make Europe the most competitive area in the world. But its formulation was balanced. It was built on three pillars given equal priority – economic, social and environmental. It stated that, for the decade up to 2010, the strategic goal of the European Union would be to become 'the most dynamic and competitive knowledge-based economy in the world', capable of sustainable economic growth with more and better jobs and greater social cohesion and protection for the environment. Progress on this agenda has been slow mainly, in my opinion, because the differences of perspectives outlined earlier have not been resolved, but rather have been camouflaged in the language of the Lisbon document.

Although usually couched in terms of sovereignty and national identity, the real question at the heart of the European debate has always been one of political economy. Conservative opinion was comfortable with Europe when its social model was a bulwark against Soviet influence, but turned against it in the 1980s when the American New Right began to assert itself.

It is somewhat ironic that the British Labour Party should be the principal advocate for liberal politics in Europe and that its main opponent should be a French centre-right politician. It is ironic not just because of political labels, but because Britain has a million civil servants more than France and a country that spends 46 per cent of its GDP on public services can hardly be considered to be on the same wavelength as the US. And yet that is the perception that clearly led the French to reject what they saw as the imposition on them of the Anglo–American model via the EU Constitutional Treaty. The force of the perception can be judged from the fact that the rejected Constitution text contained nothing to project it as being Anglo–American in orientation. It is probably the most comprehensive compendium of citizens' rights anywhere and it specifically enshrines the social market economy model. It was not as if the French did not understand this: after all, books about the Constitution were best sellers.

So what is it about the UK that so alarmed the French? Key figures in the Labour leadership peddle the myth of US superiority, but it would be wrong to dismiss their motives as right-wing. They hope that by importing US-style capitalism, Britain can maximise efficiency and growth and generate the revenues needed to raise long-term investment in public services. In other words, they want to marry a neo-liberal economy to the social democratic state.

The problem with this approach is that the economy does not form a discrete and separable sphere of human activity. Economic structures generate values and outcomes that help to shape political culture. If they result in ever-widening disparities of wealth, as they tend to do in both Britain and Ireland, the ethic of social solidarity from which public services draw their legitimacy will weaken. There are also resource and other limits to the capacity of the state to compensate for the failure of the market to provide security and a decent income when standards are constantly being driven down. The looming crisis in pensions is a case in point. On this analysis, the French were right to be wary of the Anglo model but, in truth, the picture is more complex than is allowed by the current debate in Europe.

In my opinion, the Lisbon Strategy is now moribund. It is impossible to advance it in a community of nations where opinion is polarised between conflicting visions of the future. The problem is that the advocates of the respective visions are unwilling to engage in the rigorous analysis that would give a direction to Europe. The Employment Taskforce (2003), which was chaired by Wim Kok, tried to do that in its report but this seems to be more or less sidelined. The statements of José Manuel Barroso, President of the European Commission, about the Lisbon Strategy appeared to prioritise economic growth over social cohesion and the environment. The draft Directive on Services in the Internal Market (the 'Bolkenstein Directive') no doubt helped to fuel French concerns about the Constitution. President Barroso's statement to the Lisbon Council in June 2005, in which he described opponents of the Services Directive as 'reactionaries', was ill-judged. To the extent that services are the fastest growing area of economic activity, it makes sense to legislate to maximise the potential of the sector. What does not make sense is the draft Directive's proposal to allow service industries base themselves in the low-cost eastern European EU countries and from there to export personnel to provide services in the fifteen countries that made up the EU prior to May 2004 on pay rates and conditions of employment which apply in the base country. This is known as the 'country of origin' principle. It is immediately obvious that this crazy proposition would cause fear and resentment and undermine support for the whole European project. The role played by the so-called 'Polish Plumber' in the French Referendum is testament to that. Europe also needs a clear framework within which to deal with public services or 'services of general interest', as they are called, because constant threats of privatisation of public services convey the impression that the Commission is on an ideological crusade.

It is not as if we do not know what the consequences of the country of origin provision would be. Up to the time of the GAMA dispute in Ireland, this might have been in the realms of speculation, but GAMA revealed the face of exploitation of workers in very graphic form and the subsequent awarding of more public capital contracts to that company shows how difficult it is to do anything about it – and GAMA is a construction company based in Turkey, a country not even in the EU.

At face value, Mr Barroso's agenda is of limited interest to us in Ireland. But while we have managed to make great economic progress in recent years we remain a very unequal society in terms of the division of wealth and the level and quality of our public services. The concept of a 'social Europe', first advocated by Jacques Delors and now formally part of the EU draft Constitution, and embodied in social systems of the majority of the EU 15, is what we in the trade union movement aspire to. Mr Barroso's apparent abandoning, or at least downgrading, of that pillar of the Lisbon Strategy is very disappointing. Preventing a race to the bottom in terms of employment conditions is our biggest single challenge in a globalised world and the studied attempts to undermine the concept of a 'social Europe' make it very difficult for those of us in the trade union movement who support Europe.

What of this crusade to americanise Europe? Has it any basis in empirical experience? Although the US is currently not looking very good, with its entanglement in Iraq, its twin fiscal and trade deficits, and its inadequate response to the New Orleans hurricane disaster, we should still look at the reality of the respective economic performance of Europe and the US over time. It is worth adjusting this perspective to take into account not just the current state of the continents, but also a comparison of how they have developed since the end of the Second World War. As Jeremy Rifkin has pointed out, what is so remarkable is how fast Europe caught up with the US (Rifkin, 2004). In 1960, the US economy was producing nearly two times more goods and services per hour than France and the United Kingdom. By 2002, however, Europe had virtually closed the productivity gap with the US, boosting labour productivity per hour worked to 79 per cent of the US level.

European productivity growth outperformed that of the US during virtually the entire half-century following the war. Between 1950 and 1973, European productivity grew by 4.44 per cent, compared to 2.68 per cent in the US, and from 1978 to 2000, the productivity growth in Europe increased by 2.4 per cent compared to 1.37 per cent in the US. Between 1990 and 1995, twelve EU countries showed higher productivity growth than the US. While US productivity moved slightly ahead in the last half decade of the 1990s, showing a 1.9 per cent increase in growth compared to a 1.3 per cent growth rate in Europe, seven of the EU countries still grew faster. In 2002, even with the surge in US productivity, six European countries achieved higher productivity. (As a matter of interest, the *Financial Times* reported on 13 September 2005 that figures from the British Office for National Statistics showed that UK productivity was 11 per cent behind that of France in 2004, as against 10 per cent in 2003.)

Thus it can be stated that while some European countries have problems, Europe as a whole cannot be denigrated. Moreover, performance comparisons with the US reflect differences in demographic circumstances, such as migration flows, fertility rates and population density, which have nothing to do with levels of market regulation or taxation. The biggest single contribution to America's recent productivity growth has been from the retail and wholesale sector, where consumer exuberance has kept the tills clattering away.

But, critics of Europe will say, unemployment rates in America are half those of Europe. On the face of it this is true, but closer examination reveals that the difference between the two continents on this measure is also less than official statistics allow. Consider that there are, according to Jeremy Rifkin, two million Americans so discouraged that they have dropped out of the workforce and are no longer counted in official statistics. Consider also that nearly 2 per cent of the male population of the US is in prison. The US Department of Labor put the official unemployment figure at 6.2 per cent in the summer of 2003, but if discouraged workers who have given up are counted the real unemployment figure is 9 per cent of the workforce, similar to that of Europe.

Europe's industrial base is also stronger than that of the US. When the German auto giant Daimler-Benz bought out America's third largest carmaker, Chrysler, a few years ago, it was treated as something of a fluke. But, in fact, 61 of the 140 biggest companies on the Global Fortune 500 Rankings are European, while only 50 are American and 29 are based in Asia. While Germany, as the country accounting for 30 per cent of European GDP, is the key target of criticism from pro-American commentators, it is the strongest exporting country in the world and the only one of the G8 to increase its market share in recent years.

It is against this background that the debate about the future of work in Europe is taking place. Liberals argue that high unemployment, high taxes, burdensome welfare systems and convoluted regulatory regimes will perpetuate economic stagnation. People in government, industry and civil society are locked in a fierce ideological battle about whether the rules governing commerce, employment and trade need to be reformed and, if so, how. Liberals want these reforms to bring Europe's economic politics in line with the United States.

Were the European Union to abandon much of its social net in favour of a more libertarian market approach, its 457 million people might find themselves saddled with the kind of deep social ills that now plague the United States, from greater inequality to increased poverty, lawlessness and incarceration – precisely the type of social ills so brutally exposed by Hurricane Katrina in August 2005. That would be a high price for European citizens to pay when we consider that the American model not only has failed to deliver real job growth but has forced millions of Americans into long-term debt and bankruptcy. Of course, Europeans will not pay this price. Until the political elite of Europe accepts this reality Europe cannot move on.

But what does moving on mean in practice? First of all, Europe needs to stimulate consumer demand in its major economies. Only 12 per cent of Europe's trade is external to itself. The problem is lack of consumer confidence. Europeans have to be convinced to spend more money. Confidence is a key factor, but other options are necessary too. Fiscal policy has limited potential. The European Central Bank (ECB) could reduce interest rates and its reluctance to do so reflects a flaw in the Eurozone system. The ECB's remit (price stability) is too narrow and it should never have been ceded the power it has in a single currency zone. Here we could learn something from the US. The Federal Reserve is required to consider broader economic conditions, not just inflation. In addition, to put it bluntly, Europeans need better pay rises. The extraordinary wage moderation of recent years has gone too far.

The liberal solution which favours labour market and welfare 'reform' – actually a euphemism for worsening employment security – has the effect of making people uncertain about the future and less willing to spend money. As such, it is a self-defeating ordinance. Nothing in this paper so far should be construed as a case for the status quo. The libertarian pro-American argument is, for reasons that I hope are persuasive, discredited and should be pushed to the margins of debate. Only then can a realistic and mature approach to the future be embraced. Wim Kok had good ideas about how to operationalise the Lisbon Strategy and the report, *Facing the Challenge* (2004), issued by the High Level Group that he chaired, deserved more attention than it received.

There is no one European social model to defend. The Belgian economist, Andre Sapir (2005) claims that there are, in fact, four distinct models: the Rhineland, the Anglo–Saxon, the Mediterranean and the Nordic, all with different characteristics. Underlying these different models is a broad set of social democratic values. These values hold that best outcomes do not come from markets and require active intervention by the state. In my opinion, if there is a model that can provide the optimum mix of economic dynamism and social justice for Europe to succeed it is to be found in Scandinavia. In recent years, as Wim Kok points out, the Scandinavians have combined healthy growth, low unemployment, rising productivity and large export surpluses with some of the lowest levels of inequality in the world. Moreover, a strong welfare state and a framework of social bargaining that involves trade unions are the mechanisms through which these countries have managed economic change successfully. According to neo-liberal orthodoxy, these are the very factors that are supposed to be holding back Europe.

The debate on Europe is about much more than constitutions and currencies. It is fundamentally a question of whether an alternative to the Washington Consensus remains possible. No one who occupies a position on the centre-left of politics should be in any doubt about what is at stake.

As mentioned earlier, at a certain level the Lisbon Strategy has but limited relevance to Ireland. Whereas only 12 per cent of Eurozone trade is external, over 60 per cent of Ireland's trade is with external markets. We have a very open economy, categorised as one of the most globalised in the world. Our main markets are outside the Eurozone and so our competitive position is much more vulnerable to currency fluctuations. Our demographic situation is much more favourable than that of the rest of Europe, in that we have a younger population. We have an economic growth rate that is three times the EU average. We have virtually full employment, low public spending and an overall low tax burden. We also have very light labour market and product regulation. We are, for example, the only country in Europe that has no statutory right to collective bargaining (even the US grants this right).

However, we are, according to successive United Nations Human Development Reports, one of the most unequal countries in the world. We have very serious public service deficits, most notably in health care, and an infrastructure of caring for children and elderly people that is almost non-existent. Our private pension schemes cover less than half the population and those that do exist are woefully inadequate. We spend less than anyone else in Europe on social transfers and our public expenditure is only 34 per cent of GDP by comparison to an average of 37.5 per cent for the Eurozone countries. In short, we are very much part of the Anglo-American group of nations except in one respect – we have embraced the European approach to social dialogue.

The question is, do we want to stay where we are? To be sure, we would be crazy to abandon what works for us but we cannot live indefinitely with the social deficits I have described earlier. It is already clear, for example, that health care and child care are major political issues that no government or prospective government can ignore. In time, too, the consequences of an ageing population, inadequate pensions provision and the fact that Irish workers, albeit on a lower income tax (but not direct tax) regime, have to shell out their wages on things that their fellow European citizens get for free as part of the social wage, will hit home. Behind it all, the greatest threat to our well-being lies in the erosion of social cohesion that will certainly happen if we continue on the trajectory we are now on.

One day soon, Ireland will have to choose what sort of a country it wants to be – not so much Boston or Berlin, more like Chicago or Copenhagen. To the extent that Europe's future prosperity is linked to the Lisbon Strategy it matters to us what happens to it. I believe passionately that Ireland's future lies in a more deeply integrated Europe. A Europe that is successful, that can engage with a globalised world without sacrificing the welfare of its citizens in some kind of Darwinian race to the bottom. A Europe that stands for civilised values, a Europe that can influence the world by use of soft power as it has in the Balkans and Iran. If Europe can manage its way through its current difficulties then, with confidence restored, perhaps we can resume our journey towards the vision set out by Monnet all those years ago.

Note

1. This paper was presented at the conference, *The Future of Europe: Uniting Vision, Values and Citizens?*, held in Dublin on 27 September 2005.

References

Ducêne, François (1994) *Jean Monnet: The First Statesman of Interdependence*, London: W.W. Norton & Co.

Employment Taskforce (2003) *Jobs, Jobs, Jobs: Creating More Employment in Europe*, Report of the Employment Taskforce chaired by Wim Kok, Brussels: European Commission. (www.europa.eu.int/comm/employment_social/employment_strategy)

Facing the Challenge: The Lisbon Strategy for Growth and Employment (2004) Report of the High-Level Group chaired by Wim Kok, Luxembourg: Office for Official Publications of the European Communities. (www.europa.eu.int/comm/lisbon_strategy/index_en.html)

Rifkin, Jeremy (2004) *The European Dream: How Europe's Vision of the Future is Quietly Eclipsing the American Dream*, Cambridge: Polity Press.

Sapir, André (2005) *Globalisation and the Reform of European Social Models*, Background document for the presentation of ECOFIN informal meeting, Manchester, 9 September 2005, Brussels: Bruegel. (www.bruegel.org)

The Market as a Mechanism for Social Justice

The Case of Europe[1]

Dan O'Brien

Citizens of the European Union have never been more prosperous than they are today and have never enjoyed such a range of rights and liberties. They inhabit an unusually safe corner of the world and have never lived longer or healthier lives. The appeal of life in Europe can be seen in the number of immigrants it attracts and by the desire of almost every non-member country in and around Europe to join the EU.

Despite this, Europe is suffering a crisis of confidence. The rejection of the EU Constitutional Treaty by French and Dutch voters in mid-2005 came at a time of growing concerns about the region's economic performance. Over the past decade, the EU has not matched its potential, not matched the strong rates of economic expansion enjoyed by the US and not come anywhere near matching growth in the most dynamic parts of the developing world, notably China and India. Confidence has been further eroded by failing efforts at EU level to raise the continent's game in the shape of the ambitious Lisbon Strategy. Extrapolated into the future, current trends would see a decline in Europe's importance in the world. Pessimists warn that the continent could become a stagnant backwater. Many argue that the European economy is afflicted by terminal sclerosis and, relatedly, that the welfare state is no longer affordable.

Such claims lack perspective, and, happily, neither of these latter two gloomier assertions is correct.[2] On the first count, while it is true that some European economies have serious problems (for example, Germany and France), many do not (Ireland and the Nordics) and of those that do, only a small number (Italy and Portugal) face profound challenges (and, for comparison, even these latter countries have fewer and less serious problems than Ireland in the 1980s). But not only is the European economic picture mixed and declinist talk much exaggerated, Europe's many strengths have been understated: the continent's workforce is highly educated; its physical infrastructure unbettered globally; its currency strong and stable; its balance of payments with the rest of the world sustainable; its companies in many of the most important sectors world-beating.

The essentially solid economic fundamentals of the EU and its continued high levels of wealth creation mean that there is nothing inherently unaffordable about the level of European social spending, and claims about the demise of the welfare state are, at best, premature.[3] Another reason to believe in the sustainability of the welfare state is that much (but not all) of the resources allocated to creating and maintaining European countries' social safety nets actually contribute to better economic performance by reducing the costs of risk taking. This boosts wealth-creation by, for example, increasing business start-ups and encouraging the movement from secure jobs to less secure but more rewarding ones.

None of this is to say that Europe does not have serious problems which need to be addressed. But here, too, there is reason for optimism. By and large, governments are fully aware of their economic weaknesses and there is general consensus in most countries about what needs to be done. Limited success in moving ahead has more to do with the strength of opposition from those who may be negatively affected and the political weakness of many governments than with disagreement about what the problems are and how to address them.

Ideology is Dead: Long Live Evidence-Based Policy-Making!
The demise of old-style left–right ideology is to be thanked for the broad consensus on the European reform process, as embodied in the Lisbon Strategy. While evidence-based policy-making has always played a greater role than ideology in Europe's democracies, it has triumphed since the collapse of communism and the subsequent failure of experiments in ultra-minimal government in former communist countries. Today, serious thinkers and commentators agree that the secret of economic success is to have both well-

functioning markets *and* well-functioning states, because when they both work they become mutually reinforcing. Nowhere is this to be seen more clearly than in thinking in the field of development economics. The watchword among the policy and scholarly communities is now 'good governance', that is, an effective and efficient state is essential if market economies are to generate the sort of wealth that can lift people out of poverty and towards prosperity. A non-ideological analysis of economic history supports this: almost every country in the world that today enjoys high standards of living has achieved success by a combination of market and state working in tandem. Ireland is no exception: the role of the state in supporting foreign multinationals to create jobs, widen the export base and generate tax revenues is a textbook example of smart government.

When one considers what governments actually do today (ignoring their spin), left–right ideology plays little role. Socialist governments liberalise and privatise, while governments on the right increase taxes and add to environmental protection legislation. When countries consider how to organise their education systems, social welfare benefits, health care, pensions and transport, they assess what has worked in existing policies, they examine what has failed and why and they look at international experience. (In the EU, a system of peer review is designed to tease out best practice so that policies that work in one country can more easily be assessed for suitability in others.) At EU level, legislation and policy choices traditionally associated with both left and right are the norm. It is, incidentally, for this reason that ideologues on the right can find evidence to support their paranoid view that the EU is a plot to impose socialism on Europe by stealth, while their counterparts on the left can simultaneously point to things that support their equally paranoid charge that the EU is a neo-liberal conspiracy for the benefit of rapacious multinational corporations.

So what can Europe's countries do to solve the problems they face and put their economies and welfare systems on a firmer footing for the future? Solutions are (and should be) both market-centred and state-based. Of the latter, there are plenty of good proposals about, with many forming part of the Lisbon Strategy, including greater public investment in education and training, more expenditure on research and investment, and the implementation of the EU's Environment Technology Action Plan. But for the EU as a whole, the direction needed today is, on balance, towards more market. Not only will this help strengthen economic growth, it will make for greater social justice. In three of the most important areas – jobs, food prices and the freedom to compete – more market and less state intervention will make a more prosperous *and* fairer society.

Worker Protection: A Fine Balance

While high unemployment in Europe is confined to a minority of countries (over the past decade just six of the EU 15 have had levels of joblessness averaging above 8 per cent), it afflicts most of the big economies – France, Germany, Italy and Spain. Given the number of people affected, there is almost universal consensus across the political spectrum that this is Europe's major socio-economic failing. It is not hard to see why. Joblessness means not only material deprivation: it deprives people of dignity, of social interaction, of self-reliance and of hope for the future. In those countries afflicted, the young are particularly badly affected, with up to a third of people under thirty suffering the frustration of spending their youth in a vain search for employment.

Why, then, are some countries successful in generating employment and others less so? The answer lies mostly in how governments intervene in their labour markets. While too little protection for employees means unnecessary insecurity, the social harm caused by excessive regulation can be just as great. Though this may sound counter-intuitive, the injustice of over-protection is incontestable. Excessive employment protection legislation (EPL) means that, because it is very difficult or very costly to lay off workers, employers hire fewer people. The evidence shows clearly that the higher the level of protection, the lower the level of employment. The result of excessive protection is that those on the inside are very secure, while those without a job have far less chance of finding one. A second injustice also inevitably flows from cosseting labour market insiders, and can be seen in all the high-unemployment countries. Where people are locked out of the labour market, desperation to find a job pushes more people into the shadow economy where wages are lower, benefits few and protection non-existent.

The Lisbon Strategy recognises all this, as did the expert group, chaired by Wim Kok and including trade unionists, academics and business people, which carried out an independent review of the measures needed to achieve the Lisbon objectives (*Facing the Challenge*, 2004). However unpalatable, those countries with high unemployment need to make it easier to fire workers. But while this may sound harsh, it does not mean a slippery slope to a Dickensian world in which people can be sacked at the whim of a boss, as is often suggested by opponents of reform. It is, rather, a rebalancing of labour law to give as much protection as possible to those in work without damaging unemployed people's prospects of finding a job. The sort of labour market arrangements many advocates of reform have in mind, including the expert group chaired by Kok, are those in Denmark, a country well-known for its egalitarian ways. The Danes recognise that economic change is inevitable and will undoubtedly bring with it a degree of insecurity. But they also recognise that this insecurity cannot be legislated away. Their system of 'flexicurity', which is seen by most to have got the worker protection balance right, has low levels of EPL, giving flexibility to employers who in a time of rapid change need to be able to restructure their companies to remain competitive. It also gives security to employees by equipping them with marketable skills and offering high unemployment benefits to protect against hardship when people are between jobs. (The evidence suggests that higher benefits do not act as a significant disincentive to returning to work.)

As in the case of many of Europe's current socio-economics ills, the answer to joblessness and its attendant injustices is to be found in allowing the market to operate more freely.

CAP: Fits Farmers, Hurts the Poor

While the importance of having a job can hardly be understated, access to food is an absolute essential. In the market for food in Europe, state intervention, in the guise of the EU's Common Agricultural Policy (CAP), is excessively tilted towards those who are doing well, with the cost falling disproportionately on those who are poor. The transfer of resources to farmers is engineered in two ways. The first is through artificially guaranteeing high prices for farm produce; this results in consumers paying higher prices for food than they would if it were imported from farmers elsewhere who can produce it more cheaply. The second is through direct transfers to farmers. This money is raised from taxing others in society, including the poor. The CAP benefits some farmers to the tune of as much as €6,000 a week, while the average family in the EU picks up the tab with, by some estimates, an extra €1,000 added to its annual grocery bill. For families struggling on low wages or social welfare, this amounts to a far higher proportion of disposable income than for richer families – a thoroughly regressive mechanism.

The effects of the CAP on the developing world are also considerable. Market intervention by Europe drives down world prices of food and causes greater price fluctuations elsewhere. This directly undermines the farming sectors in developing countries with negative effects for food supplies in those countries and for their prospects of accelerating economic development. Not only does this policy work against the development programmes of EU countries, it exposes Europe to justifiable accusations of double standards in trade policy.

Europe is not alone in the developed world in intervening heavily in its market for food. The rationale behind these systems of agricultural subsidies and protection is mostly to ensure that there is always enough food produced locally so that no matter what happens elsewhere in the world there will not be an interruption in supply. It makes sense to have a degree of self-sufficiency, and this security dimension, ignored entirely by some opponents of the CAP, remains important today in an unstable world. But Europe produces more food than it needs and exports the surplus. As in the case of labour laws, the balance has tilted towards excessive and damaging government intervention in the market for food. While the CAP has been partially reformed, the case for deeper reform is strong. The case is overwhelming when one considers CAP's regressive redistributive effects in Europe and its development-retarding effects globally.

The argument made here, therefore, is not one for abandoning the CAP, but for a rebalancing, allowing the market a greater role so that the more equitable outcome it would produce can be attained.

The Freedom to Compete: Giving Everyone a Chance

There is little disagreement that a significant reason for Europe's recent economic under-performance is a result of government-imposed curbs on the freedom to set up businesses and on the freedom of existing firms to provide goods and services where they believe there is a demand to be satisfied. While sometimes these curbs are sensible, a necessary evil, or just a least-worst solution, most are either anachronistic or exist because of the power of a lobby group to influence policy. Such barriers have a number of negative effects. First, by protecting insiders, they unjustly exclude outsiders. Second, and relatedly, they usually mean fewer jobs. Third, they always result in higher prices, impacting most on those on lower incomes. Fourth, they raise other companies' costs, thus making them less competitive.

Examples of what happens when markets are liberalised show that the outcome is indisputably beneficial.[4] While air travel was once the preserve of the rich it is now available to everyone, thanks to the opening up of the European market. Liberalisation has also transformed telecommunication – in most European countries up until the 1980s having a telephone installed took months and calls were expensive. Today, prices are a fraction of what they were and almost every adult owns a mobile phone. These benefits are now taken for granted, and it is hard today to remember just why the state banned people from freely offering these services. On a macro level, liberalisation of economic activity between countries has made Europe more prosperous, with no country benefiting more than Ireland: it can be persuasively argued that the Celtic Tiger might never have come to life if the EU's single market had not been created in 1992.

Despite the successes of liberalisation, vested interests in sheltered sectors continue to lobby against fair competition, foretelling doom for everyone if they have to compete fairly. This can be seen in the debate about the liberalisation of services which ignited in the run-up to the French referendum on the EU Constitution. Previously, the Services Directive had been an uncontroversial piece of law working its way through the EU's legislative process, being amended and changed to iron out its imperfections. Just how uncontentious it was can be seen by the endorsement given to services liberalisation in *Facing the Challenge* (2004), the report of the Kok expert group, which included the heads of the Austrian and Swedish trade union federations. Given that two-thirds of Europe's wealth is generated by services providers, the potential for creating jobs and driving down prices is great if barriers can be broken down as envisaged by the Directive.

High on the list of Lisbon Strategy reforms also is the removal of government curbs on entrepreneurship. These restrictions are to be found mostly in countries with strongly statist traditions, particularly in southern Europe, where the freedom to set up a business is severely curbed by onerous quantities of regulation and the requirement to apply for multiple permits. Jumping through these hoops takes much time, money and effort, often resulting in the exclusion of those with more limited means from setting up business. Founding a company in Greece costs a quarter of average per capita income, and in Portugal it takes fifty-four days. In Denmark, the state does not charge aspiring entrepreneurs to start a business and they can be up and running in as little as five days (World Bank and International Finance Corporation, 2006). Just as in the case of excessive labour market regulation, Europe's barriers to entrepreneuralism drive those with business ideas into the shadow economy where no regulations apply. The result is bad for entrepreneurs, bad for their employees and bad for their customers.

Markets: Much Maligned, Poorly Defended

To begin, this paper rejected arguments usually made by the ideologically right-leaning about Europe's economies and their welfare systems. To conclude, a word on criticisms often made by the ideologically left-leaning, because support for the reforms advocated above is undermined by their anti-market arguments. The three most commonly made and serious charges are that markets result in greater inequality, increased social atomisation and an erosion of standards and rights.

Inequality first. One does not need to search far to find statements such as this: 'the inherent tendency of unregulated capitalist economies [is] towards ever-wider inequalities' (Wilson, 2005). This assertion and variants thereof are repeated so frequently by those hostile to markets that they have come to be believed as true by many non ideologically-minded people. The truth about inequality, which is determined by many different factors, is that there are no iron laws. That said, some observations can be made. First, empirical evidence suggests that when countries begin to develop, relative income inequality rises, but then tends to fall (Iradian, 2005). (So frequently is this pattern observed it has been named: the Kuznets Curve.) In short, and contrary to the assertion above, a mass of evidence suggests that markets do not tend towards 'ever-wider inequalities'. Second, evidence from around the world shows that the most unequal countries (in Latin America, in particular) are those in which the market is prevented from working because vested interests have captured policy-making for their own benefit. In effect, those at the top have used their influence to kick the ladder away, preventing those at the bottom from participating fairly in the marketplace in a way that would allow them to become more prosperous. In many ways, Latin America today looks like Europe in the late nineteenth century, and it is often forgotten now that the European left then was pro-market precisely because it understood the power of a genuinely free market to break the stranglehold of the powerful, thereby lessening inequalities.

But does recent Irish experience undermine this point? There is a common perception that Ireland has become a more unequal society during the boom (shared by this writer until disabused by exposure to the evidence while researching this paper). There are only three data sources available. Data published by the Central Statistics Office found a very slight widening of income inequality between 1994 and 2000. ESRI data show a very slight narrowing over the same period. The most comprehensive and timely numbers, published annually by the European Commission, found that between 1995 and 2001 relative income inequality in Ireland not only fell sharply, but that the narrowing was by the far the greatest of any EU 15 country. The perception that Ireland has become more unequal during the Celtic Tiger years, whether perpetuated wittingly or unwittingly, is simply not supported by the evidence.

A second, frequently made charge is that market exchange atomises society, causing the erosion of social cohesion. Robert Putnum, perhaps the leading expert on causes of decline in social capital, says this of the US context: 'America has epitomised market capitalism for centuries, during which our stocks of social capital and civic engagement have been through great swings.' He succinctly dismisses the charge: 'A constant can't explain a variable.' (Putnam, 2000) Serious thinkers, such as Putnam, also recognise that market exchange, far from eroding social capital, actually enhances it. Commercial life, a vital element of civil society, brings people together to interact, cooperate, solve problems, socialise and build relationships. Few more eloquently and authoritatively make the case for the centrality of market participation than the Noble laureate and brains behind the UN's Human Development Index, Amartya Sen (1999).

A third, more moderate charge is that the globalisation of economic activity has intensified competition to such an extent that countries, whether they like it or not, must cut social provision and reduce standards to stay competitive (often described as the 'race to the bottom').

The 'race to the bottom' thesis has been around in one guise or another since international trade in industrial goods really took off in the nineteenth century. The argument goes that the internationalisation of economic activity intensifies competition to such an extent that pay, conditions and standards are driven down to levels in least protected countries. In Europe, concerns about a 'race to the bottom' have reached one of their periodic crescendos as a result of the Services Directive (and more recently in Ireland owing to high levels of immigration).

Developments in the EU over the past two decades provide laboratory conditions to test the race to the bottom hypothesis because the single market of the EU has been the greatest-ever experiment in intensifying competition among states. Concerns in France in the mid-1980s about an influx of Spanish and Portuguese workers were widespread in the lead-up to the 1986 Iberian accession. While some movement took place, the fears proved entirely unfounded. The current wave of immigration from states which joined in 2004 has resulted in larger flows of people, with Ireland attracting by far the most new arrivals on a per capita basis. But despite talk of anecdotal evidence of job displacement, full employment conditions continue to pertain in the Irish economy and there is no reliable evidence of depressed wage growth.

Nor has the intensification of competition in Europe as a result of the removal of national barriers to trade been accompanied by any decline in health and safety or environmental standards. Instead, these have increased, as EU-level legislation seeks to find a balance between different interests across the Union. As for tax levels, greater economic integration has not led to any decline, with government revenues remaining around 45 per cent of GDP over the past twenty years and the high tax countries in northern Europe continuing to levy taxes at up to 60 per cent of GDP. About all the evidence that exists anywhere to support the 'race to the bottom' thesis is a slight downward trend in corporation tax rates, which may or may not be related to greater economic integration.

Conclusion

While Europe is not in crisis, it does need to change and adapt. On balance, the market must play a greater role and state intervention should be reduced. This should not be seen as the thin end of a 'neo-liberal' wedge or a foot on the slippery slope to a society without state-provided welfare – the role of the state will remain central to improving both economic efficiency and social provision. But a strengthened role for the market is essential. The result will be a stronger economy and a fairer society.

Notes

1. This paper was presented at the conference, *The Future of Europe: Uniting Vision, Values and Citizens?*, held in Dublin on 27 September 2005.
2. The current crop of dire warnings about Europe echo faddish talk in the past about relative economic performance. In the 1980s, the US was declared structurally inferior to Japan and in the 1950s, when communist economies were outgrowing their market counterparts, capitalism was thought to be in danger of extinction. Subsequent developments showed how unwise extrapolation can be.
3. Public pensions are a possible exception over the longer term, but only in the unlikely event of governments halting reforms.
4. It should be noted that this argument is not to be equated with privatisation. Evidence suggests that ownership of firms is far less important than the competitive framework in which they operate.

References

Facing the Challenge: The Lisbon Strategy for Growth and Employment (2004) Report of the High-Level Group chaired by Wim Kok, Luxembourg: Office for Official Publications of the European Communities, 2004. (www.europa.eu.int/comm/lisbon_strategy/index_en.html)

Iradian, Garbis (2005) *Inequality, Poverty and Growth: Cross-Country Evidence*, Washington DC: International Monetary Fund (IMF Working Paper, WP/05/28).

Putnam, Robert D. (2000) *Bowling Alone: The Collapse and Revival of American Community*, New York: Simon & Schuster.

Sen, Amartya (1999) *Development as Freedom*, Oxford: Oxford University Press.

Wilson, Robert (2005) 'Wrong Policies to Build Social Capital', *The Irish Times*, 6 September 2005.

World Bank and International Finance Corporation (2006) *Doing Business in 2006: Creating Jobs*, Washington DC: World Bank.

The Lisbon Strategy

A Sustainable Future for Europe?[1]

Nuria Molina and Robin Hanan

Since 2004, there has been an especially intensive debate on what type of society we want to build in Europe and how this will affect our economic competitiveness. This debate was given particular focus by the mid-term review of the Lisbon Strategy, the EU's ten-year economic and social development strategy.

Adopted in 2000, the Lisbon Strategy was conceived to defend the European social model in a globalised economic environment (Council of the European Union, 2000). It rested on the three pillars of sustainable economic development, 'more and better jobs' and social cohesion. Environmental sustainability was later added as a 'fourth pillar'.

The Lisbon Strategy launched the 'social inclusion strategy', which included the National Action Plans Against Poverty and Social Exclusion (NAPs Inclusion), with strong commitments to 'make a decisive impact on the eradication of poverty' by 2010.

The Lisbon Strategy explicitly recognises that its elements stand and fall together. There are two main reasons for this: the type of economic strategy adopted will shape the society emerging, and sustainable economic growth depends on social success as much as social progress depends on economic success.

This inter-dependence is also recognised in the EU Constitutional Treaty. The inclusion of the Charter of Fundamental Rights as a central element of the Treaty was a significant development, since it meant according the Charter a legal force it currently does not have. Even if the existing Treaty is amended or shelved, it is important that an enhanced legal status is given to the Charter.

A further recognition in the Treaty of the inter-connectedness between economic and social development is the statement, in

Article III-117, that the EU must 'take into account requirements linked to the promotion of a high level of employment, the guarantee of adequate social protection, the fight against social exclusion and a high level of education, training and protection of human health' in defining and implementing all its policies. (The reference to 'the fight against social exclusion' was introduced 'on the proposal of the Irish government, following the intervention of the European Anti-Poverty Network at the National Forum on Europe' (Brown, 2005, p. 3).)

In early 2005, there was a strong push to re-focus the Lisbon Strategy on a new understanding of competitiveness, closer to the model followed in recent years in the United States. Instead of 'better jobs', the talk was of increasing job numbers, largely through the neo-liberal package of de-regulation, reduced wage costs, innovation, and so on. Also involved would be either the ignoring or removing of the social pillar and the fight against poverty.

This push was led by the Commission President, José Manuel Barroso. It reflected, in part, a fear that Europe was 'falling behind' major global competitors such as the US and Japan, but also the change in political balance in the European Commission and the Council.

The Commission's proposals brought a strong reaction from trade unions, NGOs and politicians from all over Europe, who grouped behind the slogan 'Save Our Social Europe' (SOS Europe).

Many European leaders – including some, such as Jacques Chirac, from conservative parties – rejected the Barroso proposals as unacceptable and argued for a continued balance between economic and social development.

In the event, the crucial Spring Council meeting of the EU's Prime Ministers in March 2005 agreed to restore much of the original Lisbon package (Council of the European Union, 2005). The Lisbon Strategy was re-organised into two 'streams' – 'jobs and growth' and 'social protection and social cohesion'. Yet again, the European social model had proven to have more life in it than expected.

So what is the European Social Model?

Although there is a great deal of talk about the European social model, there is no tight definition of the phrase. It is generally used to refer to some approaches to socio-economic planning common to many (although not all) western European countries since the Second World War, particularly:

- a high level of social protection;
- support for social rights and minimum standards;
- income distribution to ensure a measure of social equality;
- workers' rights and some type of social partnership.

Jepsen and Pascual (2005) have suggested that, in the current debates, three main meanings can be discerned in the way the term European social model is used. It may be:

- a description of common features shared by some EU Member States, albeit within different social systems, such as labour law upholding workers' rights, equal opportunities, a high level of social protection;
- an 'ideal model' based on a successful combination of economic efficiency and social justice;
- a distinctive transnational European project, based on key principles and concepts – such as the Charter of Fundamental Rights, equal opportunities for all, economic prosperity linked with democracy and participation – and regarded as a tool for building cohesion and legitimacy within the EU.

The third definition is the one which EAPN (European Anti Poverty Network) feels is worth working for. It presents a political project which requires leaders to reach beyond their national interests to defend a common EU approach which reflects public opinion.

Neither EAPN, nor, we suspect, broader public opinion would defend a European social model which perpetuates or increases the misery of the 69 million people who, according to European Commission figures, are now living at risk of poverty.

Eradication of Poverty by 2010

It is not just groups affected by or working against poverty who recognise the importance of strengthening the European social model. For many years the Eurobarometer opinion polls have shown that when members of the public are asked what issues the EU needs to give most attention to, they have consistently ranked 'poverty' and 'social inclusion' at the top of the list of concerns.

Eurobarometer polls in both The Netherlands and France revealed that fear of undermining the European social model was the main reason for the 'No' votes in the referenda on the EU Constitutional Treaty, far ahead of any issues to do with the Treaty itself. In The Netherlands, both 'Yes' and 'No' voters agreed by nearly three to one with the proposition that the result allowed for 'the negotiation of a more social Europe'.

The credibility of the European project thus depends as much on its ability to deliver on the social aspirations of its peoples as on any particular re-arranging of the Constitutional furniture.

The European Anti Poverty Network makes no apology for coming at this question from the point of view of the millions of people living in the EU who face poverty. We start from the position that a stronger social Europe is necessary and then ask how we are going to afford it. Our member organisations across Europe, whether they are made up of people experiencing poverty themselves or front-line community workers, are acutely aware that maintaining and developing high level social standards within any Member State requires a strong social Europe. People struggling hard to lift the burden of poverty from their lives do not need more excuses for the barriers which stop them participating fully in society – they need these barriers removed.

This is the main reason why the statement in the Lisbon Strategy that 'steps must be taken to make a decisive impact on the eradication of poverty' by 2010 needs to be matched by effective action (Council of the European Union, 2000, n. 32). This commitment will not be met even by the current European social model, much less by the new, leaner, meaner version which seems to be implied by some European leaders when they spell out their version of 'competitiveness'. To achieve this goal will take a decisive change of direction, led with political energy similar to that deployed by the project of monetary union or the single market, and backed by public pressure.

The decision to make 2010 the EU 'Year Against Poverty and Social Exclusion' must not mean that the EU leaders wait until then to take decisive action. Current actions and the debates on the future of the European social model must have the eradication of poverty at their core.

Quality Growth or Quantity Growth?

It is generally agreed that economic growth is a means to achieve social aims, not an end in itself. The disagreement is over whether growth will automatically eliminate poverty or whether it needs to be directed by social policies.

It is becoming more common to hear, as we heard in the 1950s, the assertion that the best answer to poverty is for the economy to grow as fast as possible. The evidence is clear that this simply does not happen. Unless economic growth is accompanied by conscious measures to re-distribute income and wealth, to ensure equitable access to income and services, to protect quality employment, and to ensure the right of people to participate in decision-making, it can even deepen social exclusion and poverty.

There is also the danger that some of the measures to cut tax and public expenditure that are being proposed to increase 'competitiveness' will actually undermine living standards, as they have already in some EU Member States.

Looking more broadly, it is utopian to think that poverty can be eliminated on a European, much less a global scale, by economic growth without serious redistribution of wealth. No one really believes that the planet's environment and resources could sustain 5 or 6 billion people at the current consumption levels of the western middle classes, much less at the levels which would be reached with continual growth. The big challenge of the future will be to ensure that the benefits of any growth are distributed more evenly so as to ensure a more cohesive society at national, European and world levels.

Building on Competitive Advantage

When we narrow our perspective from the global to the European level, we need to see how, not whether, social aims can be reconciled with maintaining a competitive position in the world. The fear of competition from low wage/low cost economies, such as China, must be met by building on Europe's areas of competitive advantage, not by trying to sell Chinese-level wages to European workers in the low-skilled sectors. If we are to follow the Lisbon goal of competing in the 'knowledge economy' of the future, we need more, not less, social policy.

This directly contradicts the 'low protection, low tax' alternative to the original Lisbon Strategy. How can we grow a knowledge-based economy in the future if a quarter of children live in poverty and have few prospects of completing their education? How can we integrate the ideas, knowledge and skills of migrants and indigenous minorities if we isolate and de-skill them? How can we maintain the social solidarity that is a key strength of the EU if we increase the gap between rich and poor?

If there is no agreement on minimum social standards and fundamental rights, there is a danger, within the EU and beyond, that investors will take advantage of the fear of becoming 'uncompetitive' and will encourage countries to offer ever-lower taxes, environmental and labour regulations and social spending. This 'race to the bottom' will benefit no one but the bigger investors in the long-run. There is no room in the EU for twenty-five tiger economies.

The Rich Possibilities of Wealth[2]

Throughout Europe, NGOs working day after day with and for people living in poverty and social exclusion have seen a persistence and in many cases a growth in inequality in income and wealth. It is evident that there has been a dramatic political failure to give priority and resources to fighting and preventing poverty and social exclusion. Rather than demonising increased wealth, however, it is important to focus on its inherent potential, which could be truly set free if the mechanisms of (re) distribution were changed.

The definition of wealth has to be questioned just as much as the definition of poverty. The term 'wealth' should not be restricted to property and assets alone – a society can also be wealthy in terms of its public goods and services. Similarly, the wealth of individuals is determined not only by their property but by what they can do and have. Individual quality of life thus depends to a great extent on full access to high-quality social goods and services.

A society's wealth needs to be regarded and distributed quite differently to the way it now is. If what counts is the 'good life' of all members of a society, a wealthy society would be one that is able to guarantee a minimum income for everyone, affordable access to social goods and services (education, the promotion of health, public transport, child care facilities, counselling centres, and so on) and solidarity in sharing risks.

Even focusing on economic efficiency itself, it is evident that countries with highly-developed social protection systems are the most competitive economies worldwide. A high social quota, therefore, is not bound to lead to an economic backlash, as is often feared. On the contrary, a comprehensive and effective system of social protection means greater freedom for individuals, providing them with a secure background against which they can adapt and adjust to changes in the economic environment. From this point of view, enlightened social policies are potentially an aid, not a hindrance, to a country's competitiveness. This is highlighted by the consistently good performance of the Nordic countries (noted for their well-developed systems of social protection) in the Global Competitiveness Index. *The Global Competitiveness Report 2005–2006* ranks Finland first in the world for the third consecutive year and all other Nordic countries feature in the top ten (World Economic Forum, 2005).

Political decisions define the quality of life for all of us. Therefore, discussions on how we want, and need, to reorganise our societies in order to guarantee a good life for all should be encouraged and we should not stop questioning the relevant decision-makers, as well as ourselves, about the kind of society we want to live in. To put it in other words: do we care or do we calculate?

A good life does not only include good health and bodily integrity but also ideas, creativity and playfulness, the ability to express emotions, to sustain good relationships, to enjoy a sense of belonging and to participate in the shaping of one's own life context. To this end, we badly need social policies within the framework of the European social model. If we think of 'affording' only in the traditional sense of the word, we will be, once again, only calculating, rather than caring in order to create a good life for all.

Conclusion

We desperately need a European social model, but we need one that guarantees access to fundamental rights for all and defends the dignity of people. Without this, the European Union project, and indeed politics and political institutions across Europe, will mean little for a significant part of the population they are meant to serve.

This is not the perspective of those representing the interests of big business. Nor is it a perspective in line with the dominant views which have informed the priorities and actions of the EU since the establishment of the present college of Commissioners.

It is evident that there is need for a new vision – one that is focused not just on economic success but equally on social development – to inform cooperation between EU Member States and institutions.

We recognise that it is not easy to respond positively to the demands of such a vision but we believe that the democratic base of the EU institutions requires that all the resources of the EU be put to trying, and to be seen to be trying, to doing so.

The challenge is to mobilise public opinion behind the call for an effective European social model, one capable of delivering the Lisbon promise to make a decisive impact on the eradication of poverty by 2010. This challenge requires a new dynamism in the leadership of the EU and this dynamism can only come from commitment to a vision and to values that are people- and planet-centred rather than derived solely from a narrow economic perspective.

Notes

1. This paper was presented at the conference, *The Future of Europe: Uniting Vision, Values and Citizens?*, held in Dublin on 27 September 2005.
2. The ideas contained in this section are from Moser (2005).

References

Brown, Tony (2005) *What the Constitutional Treaty Means: The Economic and Social Dimension*, Dublin: Institute of European Affairs.

Council of the European Union (2000) *Presidency Conclusions, Lisbon European Council, 23 and 24 March.*

Council of the European Union (2005) 'Relaunching the Lisbon Strategy: A Partnership for Growth and Employment' in *Presidency Conclusions, European Council, Brussels, 22 and 23 March 2005*, Brussels, 23.3.2005 (04.05), 7619/1/05 REV 1.

Jepsen, Maria and Amparo Serrano Pascual (2005) 'The European Social Model: An Exercise in Deconstruction', *Journal of European Social Policy*, Vol. 15, No. 3, pp. 231–45.

Moser, Michaela (2005) 'A Good Life for All' in Fintan Farrell, Michaela Moser and Alida Smeekes (eds.) *The EU We Want: Views from those Fighting Poverty and Social Exclusion on the Future Development of the EU*, Brussels: European Anti Poverty Network, pp. 40–9.

World Economic Forum (2005) *The Global Competitiveness Report 2005–2006: Policies Underpinning Rising Prosperity*, Basingstoke, Hampshire: Palgrave Macmillan Ltd.

People in Poverty

Actors in the Construction of Europe

Annelise Oeschger

> ... the very poor tell us over and over again that a human being's greatest misfortune is not to be hungry or unable to read, not even to be without work. The greatest misfortune is to know that you count for nothing, to the point where even your suffering is ignored. The worst blow of all is the contempt which stands between a human being and his rights. It makes the world distain what you are going through and prevents you from being recognised as worthy and capable of taking on responsibility. The greatest misfortune of extreme poverty is that for your entire existence you are like someone already dead. (Father Joseph Wresinski[1])

Participation of the Most Disadvantaged People – Why?

The sustained efforts of organisations and networks committed to people living in extreme poverty has brought about a much greater awareness of the need for disadvantaged and vulnerable groups and individuals to be able to participate in society, rather than remaining dependent on charitable assistance and the goodwill of their fellow citizens. However, translating participation into practice remains a huge challenge. To succeed, we have to remind ourselves just why such participation is necessary.

Firstly, participation reflects a deep aspiration of people living in extreme poverty and social exclusion to be useful to their families, to their community and to their environment. Participation is not simply a good method of integrating poor people into the community: it is a vital component of modern society. Universal participation is both the goal of democracy and the measure of its success, and it is a fundamental right. The reason we have not yet made more progress with social development is precisely because our societies have not known how to take account of the knowledge and skills of those left behind by development.

Yet, where the participation of people in poverty is expressly encouraged, at local, national or European level, it is often confined to the realm of social policy, and to eliciting information about specific problems and measures to address these, as if people living in poverty were only concerned with special measures while other citizens were expected to take an interest in the broader political process. This reflects the discriminatory attitudes which society and decision-makers can allow themselves without fear of a reaction from public opinion or from the jurisdictional authorities. If the poorest people are to participate – and that is what citizenship means – their influence locally, nationally and internationally must extend to all policy fields and to all stages in the policy process: proposal, formulation, implementation and evaluation.

Participation of the Most Disadvantaged People – How?

For the past thirty years, ATD Fourth World has been active in pursuing the issue of the participation of people living in poverty at national and European level. The publication, *What We Say Could Change Our Lives*, brings together the outcomes and lessons of experiments in participation which have been carried out in a number of European countries in recent years by ATD Fourth World, in partnership with other organisations (International Movement ATD Fourth World, 2006).

The experiences described began with ATD Fourth World's early 'People's Universities'. Joseph Wresinski, founder of ATD Fourth World, did not want those living in poverty, particularly in extreme poverty, to be considered simply as people to be instructed. He believed that, in a learning environment, they could bring their experience and knowledge into a dialogue with other sectors of society. From his own childhood experience of poverty, he knew that this dialogue would be possible only if recognised experts and academics agreed to allow their experience and knowledge to be complemented and challenged by that of people generally considered 'ignorant' by society as a whole. This sharing of experience and knowledge, leading to original ways of thinking about poverty and overcoming it, remains at the heart of the 'People's Universities' programme.

Joseph Wresinski started from the premise that extreme poverty is a denial of human rights and from the belief that people facing poverty and social exclusion cannot contribute to society's understanding and body of knowledge if the conditions favouring participation are not created. Who is better placed to understand and analyse the experience, history and daily struggles of people in poverty, than poor people themselves? Yet, while they are often the object of research and studies, they are almost never co-authors. Research into poverty and exclusion is therefore starved of a knowledge of poverty as experienced and understood 'from the inside'.

In a joint 'Fourth World/University' programme in France and Belgium, people in poverty, academics and representatives of voluntary and community groups chose five themes on which to work together:

- education and schooling;
- family life as a long-term project;
- replacing shame with pride;
- the work experience and know-how of the very poor;
- citizenship and representation.

Over two years, the participants worked on these five themes and together wrote a treatise on each.[2]

This initiative was followed by a programme bringing together social work professionals and people living in poverty. Again, the outcomes challenged many received ideas – for example, the theory of a hierarchy of human needs as proposed by Maslow. When the pyramid of needs he suggested was shown to the participants living in poverty, they were outraged: 'How can they say that culture is less important than decent housing?' The moderator asked how they would draw a model of human needs. One person stood up, drew a circle and divided it in several equal parts.

With the involvement of other organisations and groups, ATD Fourth World has organised similar meetings in a number of European countries, bringing together professionals and people in poverty in order to contribute collectively to the policy-making process in fields such as child care, education, training and employment, including social enterprise. Other projects have focused on the participation of people in poverty in the training of social workers. At the European level, from 1989 to 2001, seven 'European Fourth World People's Universities' were organised in Brussels in partnership with the Economic and Social Committee of the European Union. These have given rise to a series of encounters, 'The European Meeting of People Experiencing Poverty', the first of which was held in 2001 during the Belgian Presidency of the EU. Subsequent meetings have been organised by the country holding the Presidency in the first half of the year, working in close collaboration with the European Anti Poverty Network (EAPN).[3]

Given the extent to which exclusion has deprived poor people of vital resources, including cultural resources, a considerable investment has to be made in these kinds of joint participative initiatives. What is also needed is a fresh approach to citizenship and to sharing in society. Policy-makers have to be persuaded that investing time and resources to permit effective participation of people and groups experiencing poverty is a political necessity.

Participation *Can* Make a Difference

Across Europe, the participation of people who are poor in this kind of dialogue has already had an impact on a number of measures and policies – and on people's lives, for this is what counts at the end of the day. Courageous changes in laws and policies already obtained at a European level are a solid basis for going further. I mention just two of these initiatives here.

One is the 'Open Method of Coordination' as applied to EU policy in the field of social inclusion and combating poverty.[4] Among its core elements are the 'Common Objectives', which are ambitious because they have been strongly influenced by people living in poverty and associations and networks such as the European Anti Poverty Network that are committed to working alongside them. These Common Objectives recognise the multidimensional nature of poverty, speak of access to the fundamental right of being free of poverty, of preventing exclusion, of helping the most vulnerable and of mobilising all of society, including people who are themselves experiencing poverty. Another core element of the Open Method of Coordination is the elaboration and implementation of National Action Plans Against Poverty and Social Exclusion in all twenty-five Member States; in this, the participation of people living in poverty is an important element.

The other important European achievement in this area is Article 30 of the Revised European Social Charter, one of the most important legal instruments of the Council of Europe and ratified by most of the EU Member States. Article 30 recognises the right to protection against poverty and social exclusion.[5] A signature campaign aimed at getting this right written into international law was launched in 1982 in various countries and supported by people across the social spectrum. Thanks to countless meetings, including meetings with people in poverty, and thanks to the commitment of officials at various decision-making levels, the right was included in the Charter when it was published and opened for signature in 1996.[6] When I was recently in Baku, the capital of Azerbaijan, one of the forty-six Council of Europe member states, I was astonished to hear from NGO activists there that they use Article 30 when they are discussing Azerbaijan's future with government representatives: from the street to the negotiating table, crossing geographic and social borders on the way – that is European citizenship in action!

These two examples demonstrate a very important element of responsible citizenship, which involves informing ourselves and allowing others to inform themselves. The fact that members of national parliaments generally ignore the existence of EU policy in relation to poverty and social exclusion is a major obstacle to its efficiency and impact. To obtain adequate information is a duty of policy-makers. It is their responsibility to get the strategies translated into national and local policies that produce real improvements for people living in poverty. At a European round table meeting in Dublin in 2005, a participant who had a long history of living in poverty put it like this:

> We want things to change; they have to change. And change will take place in the future when people like politicians, civil servants and others can say: 'Yes, this is important – to find out exactly what is going on at the bottom and find out from the people what they want, what they need, what they think. Yes, it is our duty, part of our thinking, something we have been trained for, and we are going to do it. We've got to look to the bottom. If not, we are failing.'

It goes without saying that it is also the duty of citizens and associations to monitor the application of strategies and legal instruments to which their states have agreed.

Pre-conditions for Partnership

The involvement of the most disadvantaged citizens in political life, and in other fields too, is possible only through authentic partnership between them and people from other social, economic and cultural backgrounds. The creation of such a partnership touches the very roots of human nature and what it means to live together:

> To establish a partnership with someone means agreeing with him or her on the common goal to be reached. It is to build a project together and to act in concert in order to carry it through. A partnership cannot be achieved by people who do not consider one another as equals. An essential condition of a partnership with people facing poverty and exclusion is to consider one another as equals, in dignity, in rights, in intelligence and in knowledge, even if it is not the same knowledge. (Duquesne, 2000)

On the bus to the airport at five o'clock one morning, I mentioned to a fellow passenger that I was going to Barcelona, to a conference on how to improve democracy. 'Oh, I'd love to come along – I'd tell them!', she said. I asked her what she would tell them. She answered: 'Respect – that they have to start by respecting us.' Respect is the *sine qua non* of dialogue. A person's place in society is significantly diminished if he or she is not, first and foremost, respected by fellow citizens and by the authorities at all levels – parliament, government and administration, and judiciary. Once we feel respect, we can start talking and get a dialogue going – not just the old familiar horizontal dialogue between people with similar experiences and outlooks, but a vertical dialogue as well. Non-governmental organisations, churches and trade unions could make a big contribution to that vertical dialogue.

Many researchers into questions of democracy complain that the public distrusts politicians, but the reverse is also true: how far do political leaders trust the public? How do they rate their real abilities? Work needs to be done on political representatives' representation of the people they represent. Each side distrusts the other and doubts its abilities. The only way to overcome mutual distrust is to communicate – but communication has its conditions as well.

Researchers also tell us that the general public tends not to be aware of policies, programmes, ideas, principles and issues. But they should be aware that politicians and government officials also tend to know little about the way 'the people' really live, about their ideas and priorities. At a recent seminar in Kumanovo, Macedonia, the Mayor told us that he had visited the local villages to find out what people's priorities were. 'They were totally different from what we'd expected. We'd thought of giving them running water, but they asked me to find them a market for their vegetables.'

Council of Europe and Access to Social Rights in Europe

In the EU there exists no specific mechanism to facilitate the direct participation of poor people. Everything that is done, for instance in the framework of events marking the UN International Day for the

Eradication of Poverty, is the result of a long process and of the commitment of civil servants understanding the importance of this issue.

This is one reason for going beyond the European Union's vision and borders. The Council of Europe has existed since 1949 and, to its credit, assumes a constant mission of translating into practice a concern to bring in people who, for one reason or another, are excluded or absent from the usual consultation or decision-making processes. In this, it collaborates widely with European NGOs.

The report, *Access to Social Rights in Europe*, prepared for the Council of Europe by Mary Daly of Queen's University Belfast, analyses the obstacles that impede access to different social rights; gives examples of how obstacles are being overcome; identifies general principles for integrated approaches to improving access to social rights, and provides cross-sectoral policy guidelines on access to social rights (Daly, 2002).[7] On the basis of the report, the Committee of Ministers of the Council of Europe, representing its then forty-five member states, including all of the EU countries, adopted the *Recommendation to Member States on Improving Access to Social Rights* (Council of Europe, 2002).

Access to Social Rights in Europe was the result of a prolonged process, to which people committed to working alongside those living in extreme poverty made a pivotal contribution. I will summarise here some of its main conclusions from the viewpoint of the access of the most vulnerable people and groups to fundamental rights.

The different working groups engaged in the process did not start by evaluating measures or policies but by researching who, despite formal guarantees, do not benefit from social rights. The report states:

> There is compelling evidence ... that formal entitlement to a social right is no guarantee that a right will or can be realised in practice. In other words, a range of obstacles to the realisation of social rights exists. ... Obstacles extend across the chain of social rights, that is, from the form or declaration of the right,

to the processes, procedures and resources made available to effect social rights, to the situation of the user or potential user when trying to realise them.

Obstacles are of various kinds and are not unique to any one domain. ... In practice, they are interdependent and overlapping and hence to be thought of in terms of a chain of obstacles. In other words, one has to think of a spiral of exclusion from social rights. (Daly, 2002, p. 33)

The majority of the obstacles cannot be overcome by disadvantaged people on their own: in all European countries, these obstacles are just too deeply rooted.

Little by little, the members of the successive working groups involved in the process began to understand that exclusion not only represents hardship and suffering, but also a non-respect for people's rights, or a situation of being 'out of your rights', as people in poverty sometimes refer to it. And it is actually worse than this. People in poverty are not only 'out' of what is hoped for by legislators but they are 'out' of the community of recognised human beings. That is why it is crucial that the report, *Access to Social Rights in Europe*, emphasises that human rights are fundamentally 'non-majoritarian'.

Non-majoritarian means that [human rights] are concerned with each rather than all and aim to protect every individual, not just most people thereby leaving some excluded. In a nutshell, they are rights that apply to people by virtue of their humanity. Against this background, the experience and situation of the individual (potential) rights claimant is central. Claiming or asserting a right depends not just on the individual's legal position but also on the resources and capabilities that he or she has available. As well as financial resources, intellectual, social and cultural capabilities may be involved. (Daly, 2002, p. 32)

It is also crucial that the report and the subsequent *Recommendation* of the Committee of Ministers of the Council of Europe are clearly against a hierarchical classification of human needs, and thus of human rights. Such a division of human rights is unfortunately a tendency in some political environments, with civil and political rights being deemed to be more important than economic and social rights. This, however, fundamentally contradicts what we learn from people in extreme poverty. The *Recommendation* of the Council of Europe speaks of 'the indivisibility of human rights' and of the commitment of the Committee of Ministers 'to the promotion of social rights as an integral part of human rights'. (n. 8)

Very often, the so-called help or assistance provided to poor people respects neither their right to active participation in society, nor their human dignity. It is of significance that the Committee of Ministers of the Council of Europe in its *Recommendation* asks governments of member states to implement policies 'promoting access to social rights'. It says that such policies should:

> be guided by the values of freedom, equality, dignity, and solidarity; be based on the principles of non-discrimination, partnership, quality, privacy and transparency. (n. 14)

The Committee of Ministers also understood the fact that to improve the lives of the very poor, a clear political will was needed and so it recommended member states to '... devote particular attention to persons in situations of vulnerability'. (n. 14)

One day a cleaning woman at the Council of Europe said to me: 'You know, the ones who do the talking here all think human rights are somewhere else.' It is up to each of us to ensure that our values and ideals not only happen 'somewhere else', but also in the places where we serve and live, through our networks and influence.

Notes

1. Father Joseph Wresinski (1917–1988) was founder of the International Movement ATD Fourth World.
2. These are available in French. See Groupe de Recherche Quart Monde–Université (1999).
3. The second European Meeting of People Experiencing Poverty was held during the Greek Presidency (2003); the third during the Irish Presidency (2004), and fourth during the Luxembourg Presidency (2005). The fifth Meeting, organised during the Austrian Presidency, took place in Brussels on 12–13 May 2006. The theme was: 'How Do We Cope with Everyday Life?' The Meeting brought together more than 120 delegates from twenty-seven European countries to dialogue with over forty representatives of policy-makers from EU and Member State institutions. (http://www.eapn.org)
4. The Open Method of Co-ordination is a mechanism by which Member States of the EU voluntarily commit themselves to adopting coordinated approaches to furthering Union objectives. While working towards shared goals and convergence in policy, Member States retain the right to adopt the policies, practices and institutional arrangements they deem most suited to their own circumstances. It is, therefore, a form of EU governance that provides a 'middle way' between EU law and leaving policy determination entirely at national level. Application of the Open Method of Coordination can include setting common goals and timetables; establishing indicators; regular monitoring and evaluation; the exchange of information and best practices. It has been applied in an increasing number of areas including employment, pensions, poverty and social exclusion.
5. Article 30 of the revised European Social Charter states:
   With a view to ensuring the effective exercise of the right to protection against poverty and social exclusion, the Parties undertake: a) to take measures within the framework of an overall and coordinated approach to promote the effective access of persons who live or risk living in a situation of social exclusion or poverty, as well as their families, to, in particular, employment, housing, training, education, culture and social and medical assistance; b) to review these measures with a view to their adaptation if necessary.
6. The revised European Social Charter entered into force in 1999.
7. *Access to Social Rights in Europe* is available in Armenian, Bosnian, Bulgarian, English, French, German, Italian, Moldovan, Polish and Russian.

References

Council of Europe (1996) *European Social Charter* (Revised), Strasbourg.

Council of Europe (2003) *Recommendation Rec (2003) 19 of the Committee of Ministers of Member States on Improving Access to Social Rights*, Adopted by the Committee of Ministers on 24 September 2003 at the 853rd Meeting of the Ministers' Deputies. (www.coe.int/T/E/Social_cohesion/)

Daly, Mary (2002) *Access to Social Rights in Europe* (Report adopted by the European Committee for Social Cohesion, at its 8th meeting, Strasbourg, 28–30 May) Strasbourg: Council of Europe Publishing. (www.coe.int/T/E/Social_cohesion/)

Duquesne, Lucien (2000) 'Le Droit de Participer', *Revue Quart Monde*, No. 176.

International Movement ATD Fourth World (2006) *What We Say Could Change our Lives: Extreme Poverty, Participation and Access to Fundamental Rights for All*, (Prepared in the framework Community Action Programme on Social Exclusion of the European Commission 2002–2006), Paris: Éditions Quart Monde. (www.atd-fourthworld.org)

Groupe de Recherche Quart Monde–Université (1999) *Le Croisement des Savoirs – Quand le Quart Monde et l'Université Pensent Ensemble*, Collection des Livres Contre la Misère, Paris: Éditions Quart Monde/Éditions de l'Atelier.

Wresinski, Fr Joseph (1989) *Les Plus Pauvres Révélateurs de l'Indivisibilité des Droits de l'Homme* (The Very Poor, Living Proof of the Indivisibility of Human Rights), Contribution à la Commission nationale consultative des droits de l'homme, France, en 1989, Collection Cahiers de Baillet, Paris: Éditions Quart Monde, 1994. (http://www.atd-fourthworld.org)

Whose Europe?

Noel Coghlan

All is not well with the European project. An air of despondency hangs over Brussels, and with good cause. On 29 May 2005, the French voters decisively rejected the EU Constitutional Treaty. Three days later the Dutch did likewise. The unthinkable had occurred, for if the Constitution, the product of dreary days of tedious presentations and tiresome negotiations, could be so summarily dismissed by a disgruntled electorate, so too might other equally esoteric outpourings of the Brussels bureaucracy.

The reality of rejection was greeted with consternation in press rooms and council chambers alike. The acrimonious Summit that followed threw into stark relief the failure of leadership which an arrogant complacency had fostered. The European project had reached a turning point, a turning point of incalculable consequence, the trajectory of which few dared to predict. The dangers were evident, the solutions less so.

The outcome of the French and Dutch referenda stunned the political classes and shattered the culture of consensus which had enveloped the European vision. The reaction of the Council President, Luxembourg Premier Jean-Claude Junkers, who declared at a press conference on the evening of 16 June 2005, 'I want to believe in my heart that neither the French nor the Dutch have rejected, have truly rejected, the Constitutional Treaty', served only to emphasise the gap which divided the Union's leadership from its citizens.

That gap had been widening for some time. Political debate in the Union had increasingly been restricted to a narrow elite as access to key public fora, the television talk shows and the columns of the broadsheets, became a 'tickets only' affair. Developments in media technology have not made matters easier. A 'free market' ideology, which reduces public debate to a tradable commodity based on 'niche' programming, is fundamentally corrosive of democracy. All too often, the commercialisation of television has been accompanied by a flowering of channels and a withering of choice as like-minded talk to like-minded, blissfully isolated from alternative viewpoints.

Effective citizenship, whether it is at European, national or local level, depends vitally on the existence of fora in which differences can be aired and understanding promoted. The many and varied perspectives, the differing values and interests, that characterise the multicultural society that is the European Union cannot be accommodated in a commercialised media geared to the interests of the economically powerful. Quite apart from the issue of editorial independence, because it is dependent on advertising and subscription revenue, commercial television is unable to provide that broadly-based public forum which is so basic to democratic discourse.

Our leaders complain, with some justification, that people are no longer prepared to participate in the political process. But are the people offered the opportunity to participate in any meaningful manner? The debate, if such it was, that preceded the drafting of the Constitutional Treaty highlights the weaknesses of the present regime.

At their Laeken Summit, in October 2001, the Union's leaders decided to establish a Convention to prepare the ground for a basic treaty, akin to a constitution, that would chart the way forward for an enlarged Union. The Convention, it was agreed, would consist of fifteen representatives of government (one per Member State), thirty members of national parliaments, sixteen members of the European Parliament and two members from the European Commission. Moreover, the Convention was to have a Praesidium which would consist of the chairperson, two vice-chairpersons and nine members drawn from the Convention. It would be backed by a secretariat drawn largely from the Secretariat of the Council of Ministers.

The members of the Convention were, to all intents and purposes, independent of the constituencies in whose name they had been appointed. Not only did this raise issues of accountability which were to become important as the process advanced but it also had the effect of restricting the range of perspectives and viewpoints which were represented in that forum. No mechanism existed to formally ensure a report back from the Convention members, and, equally, no formal forum or structure existed through which the interests and values of the larger public could be conveyed to them. Representatives of civic society were afforded an opportunity to present their views to the Convention, but those presentations took place in a formal and highly structured environment that gave little scope for that mutual engagement and interaction that is so critical to meaningful communication.

This weakness was particularly striking in the approach of the chairperson of the Convention, a distinguished septuagenarian and Second World War resistance hero, Valery Giscard d'Estaing. An Académicien, born on 2 February 1926 to a distinguished intellectual family (his father Edmond was a member of the prestigious Institut National) and steeped in the ethos of the Third Republic and its *grandes écoles*, he has the unusual distinction of being both an Enarque and a Polytechnicien. Giscard had pursued a career of quite remarkable versatility. Awarded the *Croix de Guerre*, France's highest military decoration, for his services to the resistance in the early 1940s, elected to the National Assembly in 1956, he had served as De Gaulle's Finance Minister in the 1960s before succeeding to the Presidency of France in 1974. In 'retirement' he had been a member of the European Parliament between 1989 and 1993. In breadth and depth of experience, Giscard was clearly an excellent choice; however, the question mark which hung over his appointment related to the generational and cultural distance which separated a person formed by the experiences of early mid-twentieth century Europe from the Europe of the early twenty-first century.

It quickly became apparent that the Convention under Giscard had little time for the little man, *les tits gens*, or indeed the smaller Member States. He did not allow votes in the Convention – he, and he alone, determined what the 'consensus' of the Convention was and what its future path should be. Moreover, he was widely seen as 'a big country' person, attentive to the interventions of the British, French and

German government representatives, less so to those of the smaller Member States, an attitude which was eventually to provoke the latter into forming a caucus, led by Ireland's Dick Roche, in an effort to ensure a less partial management of the Convention's proceedings.

This cavalier attitude towards values that differed from those of secular republicanism was typified by the Convention's extraordinary reluctance to accept the fact of Europe's Judeo–Christian heritage. That heritage has shaped our culture and formed our values as no other influence has. The unique insights offered by the teachings of the crucified Nazarene, Jesus bar-Joseph, a prophet mighty in word and deed, that swept through the eastern provinces to the very heart of Rome in the reign of the Emperor Claudius, drew its extraordinary vitality from its attractive blending of the Hebrew and Hellenistic.

The Nazarene's proclamation of a world in which the righteous and the unrighteous alike might find peace and fulfilment, an inclusive community which distinguished between neither Greek nor Gentile, slave nor freeman, proved powerfully attractive to a society which was profoundly uncertain of its values. The inequities that underlay the harsh realities and insecurities of the highly polarised Graeco–Roman world were challenged as never before. From that challenge and the changes it wrought, much of our contemporary understandings and expectations, our notions of the respect to be accorded to neighbour and outsider alike, derive.

Yet, faced with requests for a formal acknowledgement of this elementary reality, Giscard, a scion of that citadel of laicism, the École Polytechnique, consistently refused to give way, preferring to dwell on the Continent's Graeco–Roman legacy, to the extent of including a quotation on the merits of democracy from Thucydides. Ironically, the religious context from which that quotation derived, a memorial service for the Athenians who had perished in the first campaign of the Peloponnesian War, appears to have escaped Giscard.

More pointedly, perhaps, one might suggest that the secularism which Giscard so earnestly pursued involves a rejection not simply of the Judeo–Christian heritage but of a much broader range of human wisdom and insight. As we survey what remains of the discarded ideologies of modernism, we are inevitably led to the realisation that the instrumental rationalism that underpinned those ideologies failed quite simply because it was unable to offer more than a partial understanding of the human condition. A post-ideological age has seen a revival of the search for a more rounded view. There has been a rolling back of the secularist vision, philosophically in the work of writers such as Jürgen Habermas, Paul Ricoeur and Emanuel Levinas, and, at the popular level, by a desecularisation which has gained a quickening momentum over the past two decades or so and is evidenced in the rise of fundamentalist movements on a global scale. Whether Christian, Judaic or Islamic, these movements express a popular protest against a betrayal of their core values which they link to the inequities, the exploitation and the spiritual poverty of secular society. Whilst one may well disagree with the particular articulation which these protest movements adopt, it is difficult to contest the basic values which they seek to protect.

Pace my mentors at the London School of Economics many moons ago, people are not merely the optimising animals which the neo-liberal paradigm proposes. Rather they are, quite uniquely, reflexive beings. They engage in various forms of interaction with their fellow beings, live narratives, interpret events, cherish aspirations, face choices and set goals. They are capable of an altruism that rises above the narrow confines of Benthamite utilitarianism, of visions that reach beyond the bounds of prepositional rationality. In doing so, they draw on a richness of wisdom garnered over centuries, if not millennia, of human experience, resources grounded in custom, in philosophy and, not least, in religious traditions.

The great faith traditions of our world, Abrahamic and cosmic, encapsulate that richness. They offer an explanation of who we are, whence we have come and whither we are bound. They provide holistic accounts of the human condition and offer insights that give meaning to life. They are embodied truths that rise above the merely abstract and the prepositional to offer guidelines for practical living. Through their symbolism and rituals, their songs and prayers, they transform the drudgery of our daily routines into something greater than those routines. Therein lies their strength and their uniqueness for, as the Jewish theologian Jonathan Sacks reminds us, respect, restraint, humility, a sense of limits and the ability to listen and respond to human distress, the qualities that assure the very stability of our societies, are not virtues that the market can be relied upon to foster (Sacks, 2002). Nor, for that matter, can we rely on the dying embers of Enlightenment rationalism, as Giscard appears to believe, for the salvation of the European vision.

The Enlightenment, on which the Giscardian aspiration to a *Europe laïque* is grounded, sought a framework of explanation that would dispel the mists of ignorance, which were perceived to lie at the root of human misery. It did not reject the notion of an all-encompassing theology but rather secularised that theology. Nature was deified and Creation replaced the Creator as an object of worship. In this new order, built on foundations provided by Benthamite utilitarianism rounded out with Ricardian economics and the ethnologies of Treitschke and Dühring, Cartesian scepticism rapidly gave way to a touching faith in the objectivity of scientific observation, and in a synonymy between knowledge and progress.

Alas, that synonymy proved elusive. Heisenberg and Popper exploded the myth of the neutral observer; Feyerabend and Kuhn overturned the notion of a science unanchored in time and culture. Horkheimer and Adorno, writing as Giscard paced the corridors of the École Polytechnique, challenged the credentials of an instrumentalist rationality. The modernist focus on prediction over explanation, and the segmentation of discourses it entailed, denied the holistic dimension of human experience. Connectivity was lost and in its place came the horrors of colonialism and slave ships, of the Holocaust and the gulags. In an age that has long shaken off its faith in unending progress, one might well question the relevance of Giscard's dated obsession with *le model laïque*.

Challenged to explain that obsession, our Taoiseach, Bertie Ahern, wryly commented: 'The French have had one revolution to remove God from their constitution and are not prepared to risk another.' His remark was apposite but left unanswered a basic question, namely the extent to which one can seriously posit a common identity when a core value of a significant part of society can be so lightly and definitively dismissed. Other values fared little better. Two ideologies dominated the Convention's debates from the outset. Both were extraordinarily reductionist. The first was the 'integrationalist' discourse. Driven by a group of MEPs led by the long-serving German parliamentarian, Elmar Brok, the integrationalists seized the opportunity provided by the Convention to fulfil their long-standing dream of submerging existing national and regional identities, and the values associated with them, in a newly-constructed 'European identity' and to restructure the Union's institutions accordingly. Basic realities were brusquely dismissed in pursuit of that dream.

As is so often the case in the European debate, the integrationalists pressed their argument beyond its sustainable bounds. That communal identities can be, and indeed frequently are, constructions of comparatively recent vintage is incontestable – all the major nation states are, in the words the cultural anthropologist, Benedict Anderson, 'imagined communities' (Anderson, 1991). But the founding myths on which those 'imagined communities' are based have been firmly buttressed by national educational systems, conscription to the armed services, public symbols and monuments, a shared language and, dare one say it, in many instances a common faith tradition.

'Dreams', Ben Sirach wrote some two millennia ago, 'have deceived many and those who put their hope in them have perished.' Alas for the integrationalist dream, there is no single all-encompassing past, nor is there a single present and future, nor can there be. Rather, there are multiple histories, often contested histories, which reflect a range of experiences and aspirations that must be negotiated within the communities to which they relate. As is the future, so too the past is in large measure a vision, a construction that encapsulates the values and visions of the particular communities who lay claim to it within a specific time and space.

Identity, if it is to be sustainable, presupposes a broad consensus on communal values – indeed the 'other' is identified by her or his perceived negation of those values. It is an organic growth, not a hothouse plant; the experience of central and eastern Europe in the post-Soviet era demonstrates only too well the hazards of artificially-promoted identities. By focusing on a single point, the institutional structures of the Union, and seeking to encapsulate the European identity in those institutional structures, the integrationists dealt a fatal blow to the cause they sought to promote.

The second dominant ideology was neo-liberalism. Based on a highly simplified economic model, that of the Walrasian market-clearing mechanism, in which a perfectly competitive and omniscient system produces an optimal solution, the paradigm's ground assumptions and epistemological foundations are, to say the least, questionable. Nonetheless, by the late 1990s the paradigm had achieved a status not far removed from that enjoyed by the alchemist's stone in the high middle ages.

The Convention, or more precisely the Praesidium, adopted the paradigm with enthusiasm and, despite strong resistance from socialist members of the Convention, led by Belgium's Anna van Lancker and Ireland's Proinseas de Rossa, gave it a central place in their draft. Pressure from the United Kingdom, backed by a dominant right-of-centre coalition in the subsequent Intergovernmental Conference, ensured that it retained that place in the final document.

The neo-liberal paradigm creates little space for the social, which it treats as a mere sub-set of the economic. Issues of social cohesion and social solidarity, of protection for the victims of out-sourcing and personal misfortune, were swept aside as irrelevant and obscurantist relics of a bygone age. Cooperation and compassion were to be discarded and in their place competition was to be installed as the structuring principle of the Union. Growth and welfare were presented as synonyms. That the appalling experience of developing countries over the past two decades had thoroughly disproved this extraordinary proposition was dismissed as an irrelevancy. The French and Dutch voters demurred.

The case for a Constitutional Treaty is strong. The further development of the Union calls for a degree of integration that goes some distance beyond that which exists today. Federalism is a viable, if not an immediate, option. Institutional reform is, by any reckoning, long overdue. The difficulty lies not so much in the vision which the Constitutional Treaty offered but in the balance which it struck between the evident need for strengthening the Union's economic base whilst at the same time acknowledging the exigencies of political and social cohesion.

The impact of the changes proposed and debated in the Convention must be explained, discussed and negotiated at the popular level. What is required is not merely assent to change but acceptance of the implications of that change. Such acceptance, if it is to be sustainable, can only come through engagement with the larger society, with *les gens quotidiens*, with the 'plain people of Europe'. Failure to do so will, sooner or later, call into question the very future of the great European project. That engagement can only take place on the basis of credible goals.

To be credible, goals must realistically address the concerns of ordinary people, concerns to which the quickening pace of change have lent a certain edge. Change, particularly the far-reaching change that has followed in the wake of the economic and cultural globalisation of the past decade, creates anxieties and calls for careful management if it is not to overflow into a destructive reaction. Promises must be plausible and relevant and suggestions of technological or economic determinism avoided, for these kinds of suggestions only increase the sense of helplessness and hopelessness that is such a pervasively corrosive feature of our contemporary societies.

To propose that the Union can ensure competitiveness and thereby maintain job security in an era of economic and cultural globalisation is at best irresponsible and at worst self-destructive. There is as yet little sign of the convergence required to ensure the effectiveness of a Union-wide stabilisation policy and, indeed, as long as fiscal policies remain a matter for the Member States and the Member States alone, the capacity of the Union to manage such convergence is, to say the least, problematic. Yet without that convergence, the economic stability upon which public acquiescence ultimately rests will remain elusive.

Moreover, the rhetoric of success upon which so much of the Constitutional debate was grounded ignores the very real constraints that the Union faces in the economic domain. Much of Europe's so-called lack of competitiveness comes not from any productivity gap inherent in its social model but rather from the lack of a mechanism through which internal disequilibria arising from inappropriate Euro entry exchange rates can be smoothed over within the present system. Those disequilibria are reflected in cost structures which are higher than they might otherwise be. Until that issue is addressed realistically, as distinct from rhetorically, jobs will continue to be out-sourced, welfare systems dismantled and public confidence eroded, as the gap between the promise and reality becomes embarrassingly evident.

In the political and cultural domains, the Union's powers are even less developed. The hiatus which developed over the appropriate reaction to the Anglo–American invasion of Iraq underscored the lack of a meaningful common foreign and security policy. The Union's inability to muster a peace-keeping force to hold the ring in the war-ravished Democratic Republic of the Congo confirmed that perception of impotence. French resistance, and French resistance alone, has ensured the survival of the once proud European film industry in the face of Hollywood's predatory onslaughts. The Islamophobia so blatantly paraded under the guise of 'freedom of expression' in the affair of the cartoons published by a Danish newspaper in September 2005 points to a disturbing incapacity to accept and respect the boundaries of a pluralistic society. Much hangs on our capacity to rise to these daunting challenges.

Europe, and more precisely the Constitution, has a pivotal role to play in meeting these challenges. But that role needs to be more sensitively formulated than has hitherto been the case. The uncertainties and anxieties of the social and economic upheaval which we are currently experiencing are moving the public discourse from one grounded in ideologies to one whose focal point is increasingly centred on identity. To the insecure and the perplexed the certainties of the known and the familiar become all-important. In contrast, the future is a domain of which little is known and much is to be feared. A paralysing sense of loss of control, of an all-pervasive economic determinism, is widespread. In such a scenario, the experiential displaces the cognitive and the question becomes not 'what Europe'? but rather 'whose Europe'?

The violence that swept through French cities in the winter of 2005 demonstrates only too clearly the frightening consequences of exclusion and marginalisation. Nor is the phenomenon uniquely French. Britain has had its Bradfords and its Birminghams, Germany its Dresdens. The London bombings of 7 July 2005, carried out by young Englishmen of Asian descent, underlined the dangers of cultural alienation and economic exclusion. As the locus of cultural and economic policy-making becomes increasingly distant and remote, as employment prospects become daily more problematic and security-driven policies more intrusive, the sense of disconnection from mainstream society encompasses an ever-larger part of that society.

Globalisation has severed the link between power and responsibility and weakened our collective moral sense. The notion of a common good has become an obsolete relic of a distant past. The ever-quickening pace of change, cultural and technological, is a profoundly disorienting experience for many people. A sense of disempowerment and alienation has spread from the immigrant ghettos of the outer estates to the homes of the *classe moyenne*. The much-abused 'Polish plumber' has become a symbol of the anxieties that accompany this sense of déclassement and deracination.

So too is the rise of populairist parties, typified by the People's Party in Denmark, the Belgian Vlaamse Blok and Jean Marie le Pen's Front National. The scapegoating of minorities, associated with the appearance of these parties in national parliaments, is a disturbing and all too common accompaniment to that alienation. These dangerous and potentially deadly trends will be reversed only when the people repossess the European ideal.

In this scenario, the functionalist incrementalism of Giscard's mentor of the early 1950s, Jean Monnet, can no longer be an option. That approach, in which a new post-war Europe was constructed through a series of technocratically conceived projects, each of which silently elided with its successor, is inappropriate to a mature and highly-politicised Union that rightly aspires to play a major role on the global stage.

War, as Clemenceau remarked, is too important to be left to the military. Likewise with the European project. The benevolent despotism of the well-intentioned 'expert' serves only to reinforce that corrosive sense of economic and technological determinism which has so undermined popular acceptance of the European vision. The Enlightenment notion that public affairs are best directed by 'gentlemen of quality', or in its contemporary expression by privately-funded 'policy centres', many of which are surreptitiously aligned to major economic interests, is simply not an adequate foundation on which to build a truly inclusive Europe.

The events of July 2005 demonstrated beyond question that issues of identity and accountability can no longer be side-stepped. The 'little people' and their concerns cannot be ignored. Solutions based on an ill-thought-through mixture of naive integrationalism and free market fundamentalism are no longer adequate. A new and more holistic vision is required, a vision that recognises and responds to the anxieties and concerns of ordinary people faced with a future beset by uncertainty and insecurity. That vision must acknowledge and encompass the extraordinary variety of the European experience, an experience that includes, dare we repeat ourselves, the Judeo–Christian heritage as much as it does that of the Enlightenment.

A Europe of twenty-five nations and twenty plus languages, of its very essence, must be a pluralist Europe. Its driving force will be shaped by those unique linguistic and cultural resources, particular to each Member State, that mould the conceptual frameworks through which its people's aspirations are formed and articulated. It will not be, and it cannot be, either monolingual or mono-cultural.

The only viable vision of the future is one that encapsulates the deeply-rooted cultural experiences and traditions of the particular communities that together form that unique community of values which comprises the European Union. In a Union that stretches from Killarney to Kaliningrad, difference and dissent are to be respected and cherished, not rejected and belittled. Simplistic reductionisms can have no place in the construction of such a Union. Neither too can one accept a 'command and control' approach to the 'management' of public opinion nor can one acquiesce in the notion that consent to major changes in the structures of our societies and the institutions through which we are governed can be manufactured through skilfully crafted PR campaigns, long on visuals and short on substance.

If the European project is to prosper, our approach must change, and change radically. The European debate calls for a willingness to differentiate, to reach out beyond a narrow elite to the alienated, to acknowledge pluralism, to distinguish between dissent and difference, to accept that Europe is a society, not simply an economy, and that its values rise above the purely instrumental and utilitarian. In the words of Hubert Védrine, France's Foreign Minister under the socialist government of Lionel Jospin, it is necessary to turn away from a 'poisonous determination to ridicule any normal expression of patriotism and to caricature legitimate, non-xenophobic reservations about enlargement'. Védrine, writing in *Le Monde* shortly before the referendum, deplored the tendency to cast suspicion 'on people's perfectly reasonable desire to preserve some control over their own destiny and identity in the face of globalisation'. It is precisely these tendencies which have so vitiated the European debate and denied the Union a vitally needed development.

As I watched Jacques Chirac concede defeat on that warm evening in late May 2005, a French friend and former colleague declared movingly, 'C'est triste alors, la France est trahie par ces propres'.

Perhaps France, and by extension Europe, was indeed let down by those in whom it had placed its trust. Perhaps my friend might have chosen an alternative expression to better express his emotion, a French proverb which says, 'il faut parfois reculer pour mieux sauter' – it is wise to pull back a little if one is to advance. Let us learn the lessons of summer 2005 and engage with the people and with their values, broader values than the purely economic and purely secular, for only thus will the European project regain the legitimacy that its sustainability requires.

References

1. Anderson, Benedict (1991) *Imagined Communities: Reflections on the Origin and Spread of Nationalism*, second edition, London: Verso Books.
2. Sacks, Jonathan (2002) *The Dignity of Difference*, London: Continuum.

European Integration

A Vital Step on the Road to a New World Order[1]

John Palmer

The massive rejection of the proposed European Union Constitutional Treaty in the Dutch and French referenda has left political parties of left, right and centre in many key EU countries divided, disoriented and uncertain about the future of the project for a more united and integrated Europe. The subsequent debate has had the virtue of requiring some answers to basic questions by all serious political players. What is the European Union *for* in the twenty-first century? How will the process of European integration impact on the different political programmes and perspectives of both left and right?

There is a widespread but mistaken belief that European integration is driven by a political elite with a secret blueprint designed to bring about a European 'super-state' for its own sake. In reality, sovereignty sharing in the EU has evolved in a more pragmatic way. Integration has been an indispensable tool for a variety of political forces – from the centre-left and the greens to mainstream liberals and conservatives – to respond to external and internal challenges and problems. Member States have resorted to legally binding collective decisions in the EU only when the problems they faced could not be addressed effectively in any other way. Acting on the basis of shared sovereignty, rather than voluntary cooperation between sovereign governments, has been the choice of last – not first – resort.

The current malaise in the EU predates the Constitutional Treaty. The European conservative political family has become increasingly uncertain about whether further European integration (or even the existing level of integration) any longer serves its policy priorities. Not only in the British Tory party but also in some of the mainstream continental European centre-right parties important 'euro-sceptic' currents have emerged. There are conservative politicians who believe that, with the creation of a European single market and other policies designed to improve European competitiveness on world markets, there is little profit in encouraging further integration. Their attitude – shared by some business leaders – is that 'we have all the Europe we need'.

There are important figures in the European Christian Democrat camp who argue that realising a serious European Union common foreign and security policy will probably require some further transfer of sovereignty from the national Member State level to the European level. They believe this may also be true for internal security or for realising the full potential of the single European currency. But within the broad spectrum of European conservatism, europhile tendencies are no longer in the ascendancy and appear to be diminishing in influence.

Creating a European *Demos*

There is support in the European liberal political spectrum for both further integration and for a serious European *demos*. But even within some liberal parties euro-sceptic voices can be heard – notably in The Netherlands and Germany. Both conservative and liberal parties across the twenty-five EU Member States also face electoral competition from populist formations well to their right. Such divisions within the broad centre-right parties on fundamental attitudes to European integration has undermined the influence which, together, they might have expected to exercise as the *de facto* majority in the European Parliament.

These developments have also weakened the authority of the conservative majority within the enlarged college of European Commissioners. This is one reason why the current right-wing (but ex-Maoist) Portuguese President of the Commission, José Manuel Barroso, has so far proved lacklustre and ineffective. The unofficial European Parliament 'opposition' – formed by the Party of European Socialists, the European Greens and the Left Socialists – have actually been able to win Parliament's support on a range of important votes including the *de facto* reshaping of the controversial Services Directive (which aims to open up an EU-wide free market in services) in ways which will protect workers' rights. In the European Parliament, the vast majority of the social democratic, green and socialist left believe that serious economic, social and environmental progress demands 'more, not less, Europe'.

The explosive character of the split over the future political trajectory of the EU was manifest in the rival campaigns on the left in France for and against ratification of the proposed Constitutional Treaty. Ironically, many of the 'Non' campaigners were happy to fly the European flag on the night the result was announced. They insisted they wanted 'more Europe – but a different Europe' in ways that must have puzzled traditional euro-sceptics in the British labour movement.

The real division in France was less within the French socialist and green parties than between the pro-European majorities in these parties and a large proportion of their natural electorates. The reasons for the big 'No' votes in both France and The Netherlands are complex. They include hostility to and even outright fear of further neo-liberal economic policies – widely seen as at the root of a loss of job security and an erosion of welfare rights. But they also include a more overt form of populist opposition to EU enlargement and more generally to immigrants (whether from within or without the European Union). These attitudes sometimes merged into outright racism and xenophobia.

Defeat for the Constitution in France and The Netherlands will not alter the existing, broadly free market strategies followed by the EU: these are legally enshrined in earlier EU treaties that remain fully in force. What the ill-fated Constitutional Treaty would have done would have been to qualify, limit or modify these free market policies with commitments to social solidarity and workers' rights – also set out in the Charter of Fundamental Rights.

The Constitutional Treaty would also have strengthened the role in EU policy-making and decision-taking of the European Parliament – the institution that has been most supportive of higher EU labour, social and environmental standards and stronger democratic accountability in European governance. That is why, for now, the *de facto* suspension of the Treaty has strengthened rather than weakened the neo-liberal camp.

Although only France and The Netherlands have rejected the Treaty to date, compared with thirteen Member States that have approved it, EU institutional reform is 'off the agenda' for at least the next two years, until after the current cycle of elections in key Union countries, culminating in the French Presidential election in the summer of 2007. The strategic question now posed for all sections of the European left – but especially the social democratic parties – is: where do they stand now on the future of the European Union? What is the fundamental purpose of 'ever closer union' in the twenty-first century? Above all, for what policy objectives is the Union still essential? The precise future shape of the EU institutions and their relationship with Member States can only be determined for the left when there are clear answers to these questions.

EU Foreign Policy

It is revealing that EU foreign, security and even defence policy played no significant role in the referenda debates. There is broad public support for the generally (but not invariably) progressive role the EU plays in world affairs. Even many among the left euro-sceptics acknowledge that the EU operates to different global values than the Bush administration. This is linked to the Union's leadership role in encouraging the global rule of law (as exemplified by its stance on the Kyoto Agreement and the development of the International Criminal Court). Is the EU beginning to fulfil an early prediction by Jean Monnet – the so-called founding father of the European Community – that 'European integration is but a stage on the road to a new world order'? Its efforts have attracted growing European public support, particularly since the rise of neo-conservatism under President Bush.

The original dynamic behind European integration was essentially about eliminating circumstances that had generated two world wars. Subsequently, it was about the creation of a single internal market (and flanking support policies) designed to act as a springboard for European companies to better compete on world markets. Today, the most potent pressures pushing the EU towards further sovereignty sharing have primarily to do with the contradictions and the potential of ever-greater global interdependence.

The EU needs further integration in foreign and security policy if it is to sustain its leadership role in creating a global system of peace and security and as an influential advocate for a global system of governance based on democracy, social justice and economic sustainability. For as long as the twenty-five (current) EU Member States pursue separate national agendas, there can be no effective challenge to *de facto* United States hegemony. Indeed, why should Washington (or Moscow or Beijing) take the EU seriously if it is incapable of forging such a common strategy?

Towards a Democratic Global Governance

A democratic system of global governance cannot be a matter for the EU alone. But other regions of the world are beginning their own process of trans-national cooperation and (potentially) integration. Witness the remarkable development of both the Association of South East Asian Nations (ASEAN) and the putative Asian region now being debated between ASEAN, Japan, South Korea, China and (most recently) India. Note also the emergence of Mercosur (Brazil, Argentina, Chile, Paraguay and Uruguay) and its developing links with the Andean nations. The African Union is beginning to play an important role in that continent. The EU is both a source of inspiration and a key benchmark for these countries as they struggle to integrate and thus redress the political imbalance in decision-making power from which they suffer – not least in the UN Security Council and the Bretton Woods institutions.

These developments should encourage European progressives to formulate a clearer strategy for European foreign and security policy, for United Nations reform and for further development and democratisation of the institutions of global governance. Put bluntly, the cause of the left in the years ahead will depend critically on the creation of effective political instruments at both European and global level to implement policy priorities. This is not just about global strategy for peace, democracy, human rights and development. It also goes to the heart of future policy for jobs, growth, social equality and sustainable economic development.

This is not about how globalisation can be evaded or reversed (as many of the 'nationalist' left propose) but rather how globalisation can be better managed and regulated to ensure that enlightened social and political values prevail. In the longer run, this should aim at a new model for global economic development that creates a growing space for democratic, mutualist, cooperative and other non-capitalist forms of fair trade and social enterprise alongside a continuing market economy dimension.

It became obvious in the early years of the communist movement that it was not possible to achieve socialism in one country. In the past fifty years it has become equally evident that sustaining enlightened social democracy in one – or even in a small group of countries with relatively little weight within the world economy – is increasingly problematic. The history of Britain's New Labour experiment in the past decade is a case in point. Whatever the failings of the continental European economies – notably those of France and Germany – very few want to emulate a variant of the Anglo–American economic model. The widening gap between rich and poor, the still backward state of the public infrastructure and many public services, as well as the low savings rate and high rate of indebtedness, are all regarded as characteristics of the British economy that others wish to avoid – even though it is conceded there are lessons to be learned from the UK record in encouraging new business start-ups and encouraging long-term unemployed people into work.

The Nordic countries offer a far more persuasive benchmark for progressive EU governments looking for a way out of stagnation and high unemployment. Interestingly, Finland is the most competitive economy in the world (according to judgements by the World Economic Forum and the OECD) while Denmark and Sweden follow close behind. No one would contest these countries' success in maintaining high levels of welfare and sustainability. But, of course, their readiness to use a large, though efficient, public sector, properly-funded through re-distributive forms of taxation, is critical to what they have achieved.

That said, there must be a question mark over the longer-term sustainability of the Nordic economic and social models. In an expanding internal EU and world market, capital inevitably looks to move to countries with a less constraining commitment to social solidarity, weaker trade unions and less commitment to environmental sustainability. Warnings that existing EU-wide social and environmental standards may be at risk from the new global competitors (above all in Asia) in a world economy with weak or non-existent global standards and regulation are well-founded.

European democrats will want to explore ways of improving competitiveness that do not threaten their wider economic, social and environmental agenda. A critical element in the Nordic success is serious investment in education and skills, allowing enterprises to trade up rather than trade down. But there are limits to this approach. It is essential that Nordic standards become European standards and, moreover, that European standards over time gradually become global standards.

This is about much more than merely balancing economic opportunity against social and environmental costs. Again, Nordic experience illustrates that investment in both environmental protection and social and welfare standards can be justified by entrepreneurial opportunity in the increasingly wealthy new industrialising countries – particularly in Asia. They have not had the time to accumulate the knowledge, systems expertise and administrative traditions to deliver these policies effectively at home. That is why Europe's social values are global assets, not global liabilities, in the longer run.

The European Union's economic and social model (more accurately *models*) will be at risk unless, progressively, minimum social, labour and environmental standards become the global norm. At present, we have a grossly inadequate patchwork of global agreements on human rights, including specifically labour rights, social welfare and environmental sustainability. The architecture of global governance has massive gaps in its coverage. Think only of the limited recognition of Kyoto and the lack of effective links between the World Trade Organisation (which does have some effective teeth) and the International Labour Organisation (which has virtually none).

In summary, progressive policy priorities at the European level and at the global level demand a strengthening of the policy-making and decision-taking institutions of the Union. But popular political support for such a strategy will remain problematic for as long as EU institutional reform is seen only in terms of strengthening the executive powers of governments – whether they are exercised through the EU institutions or through inter-governmental cooperation at the European level. That is why a revised Constitutional Treaty must radically strengthen the modest promise of a European *demos* in the existing text.

Changing the Proposed Constitution

When a new text is eventually put forward for debate it should include two major changes to the present text. The first is to take out – and treat quite separately – all the purely policy issues which were incorporated from the earlier EU treaties. Questions about what kind of social market economy the EU should espouse or strategy for economic reform as well as social solidarity and environmental sustainability should have no place in a constitution. These matters should be agreed between the Member States but they should be capable of being amended more easily than the provisions of a Constitutional Treaty, as and when circumstances change.

There must also be a massive injection of democracy into the EU decision-making system. Accountability in relation to European issues by national governments to their national parliaments should be strengthened. But this should not be confused with making EU governance collectively more democratically accountable. A major extension of democracy at the EU level is essential not to rival but to reinforce democracy at the national, regional and local levels.

The discredited Tammany Hall style system where Member State governments haggle in secret over the appointment of Presidents of the Commission should be scrapped. The emerging European political parties should not only present clear-cut European policy programmes for European Parliament elections but also their proposed candidate for the Commission Presidency. At present, European Parliament elections suffer from acute political malnutrition: they are not about enough. There is also a case for direct popular five-yearly election of the proposed President of the European Council, who should improve coordination between Member States in areas of policy decided by cooperation rather than through legally based shared sovereignty.

The new treaty should also build on the proposals in the present text that require the Council of Ministers to take legislative decisions in public, not behind closed doors. In future, the Council of Ministers should become a kind of European Senate representing the interests of the Member States. In these circumstances, the current monopoly enjoyed by the Commission over legislative proposals might be shared with the European Parliament and – under precise conditions – with a 'citizens' right of initiative'.

All of these steps represent a 'politicisation' of the EU decision-making system, especially the role of the Commission. A covert politicisation is already a fact of life. But it is not one that gives the citizen a sense of real ownership of the decisions that set the strategic direction of the Union. Until voters are offered serious political *choices* about the economic, social, security and foreign policies of the EU, the five-yearly elections to the European Parliament will attract diminishing turnout. But it is essential that the emerging European parties not only present their competing programmes for the EU: they must also invite support for the political leadership of the EU executive.

Differentiated Integration

A future constitutional settlement must also recognise that, in a Union of twenty-five Member States (and probably many more in future), there is a limit to the 'one size fits all' approach. Subject to agreed rules, groups of countries who wish to move further and faster down the integration road should be free to do so – always keeping the door open for late developers to join. For the left, it is urgent to begin with greater integration of macro-economic policy among Member States in the euro currency area. At present, euro zone policy is dangerously over-dependent on monetary policy and the decisions of the European Central Bank.

Conclusion

The emergence of a European *demos* will, of course, take time. A European political culture will develop as electorates come to recognise what is properly the business of the different levels of European governance. After all, there is already widespread understanding in Scotland about the nature of the business of Edinburgh and of the 'federal' Whitehall and Westminster bodies. Over time, politicians will become 'European' in addition to being just 'national' personalities. Above all, such reforms are vital to kill off – once and for all – the perception that the European Union involves being governed by an 'unelected bureaucracy'.

The democratisation of the EU system will be seen by some as 'federalism by stealth'. In reality, it is about ensuring that democratic politics at the European level catch up with the changes in the real world. Indeed, this debate about democratic governance at the European level itself prefigures the coming debate about how to strengthen and democratise global governance. People do understand the realities of deepening global interdependence. But they fear the process will be at the expense of their hard-won democratic and social rights. That is why democrats have no option but to raise the banner of a democratic Europe leading the way to a democratic world. Ireland's democrats should take the lead.

Note
1. This paper was presented at the public meeting, *Europe's Role in the World: Globalisation and Global Institutions*, held in Dublin on 24 October 2005.

Europe's Role in the World[1]

John Gormley TD

Nothing highlights the growing gap between the European elite and the European citizen more than what each see as priorities. Europe's role in the world is a subject that increasingly obsesses the political and intellectual class but holds little fascination for the European citizen. It is not a theme that comes up 'on the doorstep', as we politicians like to put it. Likewise, it will hardly register in focus group discussions. Yet, in the run-up to the referenda on the European Union Constitutional Treaty in France and The Netherlands, and in the aftermath of its rejection, Europe's elite has focused relentlessly on this theme and argued that Europe's role and identity can be forged on the world stage when we have a European constitution to guide us.

The refrain from elite circles for decades has been that Europe is an economic giant but only knee-high in political terms. The European Constitution, it is contended, would provide the vital growth hormone to give Europe that necessary political muscle to take its rightful place on the world stage. Elites too often believe in quick fix, top-down solutions. Many in the political class would privately argue now that it was an error of judgement to allow the draft Constitution to be put to the people in certain Member States. A proposal I drafted at the Convention on the Future of Europe for a European-wide referendum, to be decided on the basis of a dual majority of Member States and EU citizens, was roundly rejected. Interestingly, many of those opposed to the proposal now recognise that it offers a possible way out of the morass in which the project currently finds itself.

Are we really to get a new Convention and new Constitution or is the plan simply to re-jig the existing draft, perhaps leaving out the ridiculous Part Three, 'The Policies and Functioning of the Union', and giving it back to the French and Dutch for re-consideration? That would run counter to the spirit underpinning the making of the Constitution, that is, bringing Europe closer to the people, as the Laeken Declaration recommended. There cannot be a European identity until we properly empower the European citizen. There were, of course, some provisions in the European Constitution, including the 'citizen's initiative,' which moved in the right direction, but we need to go further. There is a way forward. Following the period of reflection and dialogue, we need to establish a new Convention and draw up a new Constitution, which puts the citizen and his or her aspirations at its heart.

What Type of Europe?

What type of Europe does the European citizen want? I believe that the majority of citizens would like a Europe which is a bulwark against globalisation, not a vehicle for it, a Europe built on social protection and ecological sustainability, a Europe which does not copy the mistakes of the United States of America. For many in Europe, the Iraq war highlighted the differences between Europe and the United States. So much so that Jürgen Habermas and Jacques Derrida (2003), in an essay published simultaneously in Germany's *Frankfurter Allgemeine Zeitung* and France's *Libération*, identified five attributes differentiating Europe from the United States: the neutrality of authority, embodied in the separation of Church and State; a trust in politics rather than the capitalist market; an ethos of solidarity in the fight for social justice; high esteem for international law and the rights of the individual; support for the organisational and leading role of the state. According to Habermas and Derrida, Saturday, 15 February 2003, the date of the huge marches against the Iraq war, represented the 'birth of a European public sphere', evident on the streets of 'London and Rome, Madrid and Barcelona, Berlin and Paris'.

The clear implication was that with a common foreign and security policy Europe could act as a political and moral counter-weight to the USA. Many in the European left also have put forward the proposition that a European common foreign and security policy could have ensured the avoidance of war. There is, of course, one central problem with this argument – the majority of EU states were *for* the war. Yes, some of 'old Europe' – to use the phrase employed by Donald Rumsfeld, US Secretary of Defense – were opposed to the war, but there were many who signed the declaration of support. If it had come down to a decision to be made by a qualified majority vote on the issue, European soldiers could easily have found themselves on the bloody streets of Fallujah, or victims of car bombings, part of a counter-productive invasion and an illegal occupation. Habermas correctly states that European citizens marched on the streets of the EU capitals in opposition to the war, but their respective governments paid little heed to them – the best example of a democratic deficit.

I have no doubt that Europe's citizens would like to see a European Union that plays a positive role on the world stage. But do they really want to see a flourishing EU arms trade? Do they want to see EU troops going to war without a UN mandate? If Europe is truly to be the alternative to the 'hegemonic unilateralism' of the US, then it should recognise first and foremost that the UN – flawed as it is – needs to be reformed, not gradually abandoned.

The Solana security doctrine, and the conclusions of the Defence Working Group of the Convention for the Future of Europe, speak about the 'new threat', referring to global terrorism. The citizens of Europe might well wonder how investing in Euro-fighter and other military hardware will prevent misguided youths exploding homemade devises in the London Underground. New threats require new solutions, not old Cold War rhetoric. The proponents of European unilateralsim argue that the massacre at Srebrenice shows why the UN must on occasion be ignored. It was the feebleness of the UN, they argue falsely, which led to this attempt at genocide. It has never been made clear how an EU force consisting of Dutch troops and a French General, who failed inexplicably to call in close air support, could have acted any differently. Successive EU treaties have provided for the further militarisation of the European Union. The latest initiatives include the Armaments Agency and European

Battlegroups, seen as a forerunner for a European Common Defence. The European citizen may want to see greater cooperation between Member States in the area of defence, but would draw the line at unilaterist adventurism and increased arms spending which would undermine the European social model.

Protecting the European Social Model

It is in the protection of the European social model that the European citizen feels most left out of the equation. This feeling of alienation from the perceived neo-liberal agenda manifested itself during the debate on the EU Constitution in France and latterly in the demonstrations on French streets against new employment legislation. Increasingly, the EU is seen as the conduit through which the neo-liberal social and economic model is being institutionalised in Europe. Even a staunch supporter of the project, sociologist James Wickam, has summarised the situation thus: 'far from protecting the European social model from globalisation and/or Americanisation, the EU is at the moment busily undermining it.' (Wickham, 2002, p. 1)

Wickham goes on to say:

> Increasingly, the Commission has been removing national barriers to competition within the EU, sometimes even opening up markets, such as in postal services or electricity supply, which hardly existed before. Increasingly, when companies wish to enter what they consider a protected market, they appeal to the Commission over the head of the national government ... Increasingly, too, public services such as transport are being 'opened up' in the same way, partly by rulings of the European Court of Justice. This parallels negotiations that are going on at the international level in the World Trade Organisation (WTO), so that very soon it may be possible for companies to use the same strategies to enter national markets in health and education. Finally, the Commission has been clamping down on national state-aided companies. (p. 10)

There are many on the left who argue that the Charter for Fundamental Rights is the counter-balance to this trend. It is still not clear, however, whether social and environment rights contained in the Charter are fully judiciable. They certainly ought to be. My position on this matter is unashamedly integrationist. There are policy areas such as environmental protection and energy where more integration and big thinking are urgently required, given the scale of the challenges we now face.

Consultation and Empowerment

What is the big idea? Is it to deepen and widen the Union? Without regard to the views of the citizen? The new Constitution must provide for greater empowerment of and greater consultation with the citizen. The steps proposed by Democracy International, a network of European NGOs promoting direct democracy, which first suggested the ideas of a European Citizens' Initiative and European-wide referendum, deserve our support. Democracy International has argued that one of the principal reasons for the failure of the Constitutional Treaty is people's lack of trust in the EU institutions, which are often perceived as aloof and remote. It has made a number of key recommendations:

- Direct election of Convention members: This may not be possible in all countries but certainly a wide spectrum of views from each Member State should be represented at the Convention.
- A democratic Convention procedure: the Praesidium must be elected by Convention members, and votes – even indicative votes – should be taken.
- Ongoing citizen participation: Individual citizens, citizen groups and NGOs, etc, should be able to present proposals to the Convention, which then should be taken into consideration.
- Open outcome: the main task of the Convention should be to analyse different options and work out a solution that could command a majority among the citizens of Europe. A constitution is just one option among other possible new arrangements for the future of Europe.

- Referendum on the final proposal: the proposal worked out by the Convention must be subject to a European-wide referendum in each of the Member States to be held on the same day. The proposal would be carried if the majority of citizens and Member States agreed to it. Thresholds for these majorities would have to be worked out at the Convention.

But even before we get to that stage, Democracy International believes that trust between the European institutions and the European citizen can be re-established through the introduction of the European Citizens' Initiative. Democracy International is campaigning for the introduction of a European Citizens' Initiative by regulation into European law. In order for the Citizens' Initiative to work, the regulation must be designed in a citizen-friendly way and it will be publishing guidelines as to how this can be ensured. In its campaign literature, Democracy International states:

> The time has come for the European project to be driven by the people, and not only by an elite. When implemented, the ECI will be the first transnational tool of democracy. It will give citizens a right of initiative that is equivalent to that of the European Parliament, and much more effective than the current European citizen's right of petition. Being issue-focused, the right of initiative will contribute to shaping an open European public space around key debates that reflect citizens' real concerns. In other words, the ECI will not only help to close the gap between citizens and institutions, but also foster the development of a European civil society. (www.democracy-international.org)

It would indeed be a bold and imaginative move if the European Commission were to accept these proposals. It would certainly mean that a future European Constitution, or similar document, could be far more readily acceptable to the citizens of Europe. It would show that those in the higher echelons had finally recognised that Europe's true voice is the voice of its people.

Note

1. This paper was presented at the public meeting, *Europe's Role in the World: Globalisation and Global Institutions*, held in Dublin on 24 October 2005.

References

Habermas, Jürgen and Jacques Derrida (2003) 'Nach dem Kreig: Die Wiedergeburt Europas' ('After the War: The Rebirth of Europe'), *Frankfurter Allgemeine Zeitung*, 31 May 2003.

Wickham, James, *The End of the European Social Model: Before it Began?* Originally published as Appendix II of ICTU's submission to the National Forum on Europe, 30 January 2002. This version dated 8 October 2002. (http://www.tcd.ie/ERC/observatorydownloads/Social%20Models.pdf)

Leadership in Development

A Role for Ireland, A Role for Europe

Olive Towey

> In an age when 'history moves with the tramp of earthquake feet', in an age when a handful of men and nations have the power literally to devastate mankind, in an age when the needs of the developing nations are so large and staggering that even the richest nations often groan with the burden of assistance – in such an age, it may be asked, how can a nation as small as Ireland play much of a role on the world stage?

This question was asked by US President, John F. Kennedy, on his visit to Ireland in 1963. In his address to Dáil Éireann, he spoke of the role of small nations and of Ireland in particular – of its unique history and heritage, of its place in Europe and at the UN, of 'its remarkable combination of hope, confidence and imagination'.

His words remain today as inspiring as they are challenging. Over forty years later, in a 'transformed' Ireland, we can ask this demanding question once more: 'How can a nation as small as Ireland play much of a role on the world stage?' And in asking this question of Ireland, we are implicitly asking questions about Europe's role in the world. As Irish and as European citizens, we have the right, indeed the responsibility, to seek answers to these questions.

Ireland – Long-Held Values and Future Vision

The recent transformation of Irish society has been staggering. Ireland may be geographically on the periphery of Europe, but its membership of the EU has been central to these changes.[1]

Now one of the most globalised countries in the world,[2] Ireland's technological competences, levels of education and recent economic advancements are the envy of many. Irish society is becoming more internationally aware and more culturally enriched. However, as it enjoys the diversity, affluence and choice the 'Celtic Tiger' has brought, it must also try to address the less positive consequences of economic growth and deal with challenges such as alienation, disaffection, racism and inequality.

This period of rapid change presents endless questions: What kind of Ireland do we want to build for the future? What does it mean to be one of the most globalised countries in the world? How are our traditional 'shared values' relevant to society today? How does history inform our engagement with Europe and the wider world? How does it shape our place in that world?

Across Europe, too, a debate about visions and values gathers pace. In light of failed referenda on the European Constitution in France and The Netherlands, a 'period of reflection' has been called for, during which governments have been asked to debate with citizens what future they want for Europe – a union of twenty-five diverse though united countries.

What better time to consider – with hope, confidence and imagination – the big role this small nation can play in Europe's future? Out of our long-held traditions and values, out of our interconnectedness with countries far beyond our borders, we have a unique opportunity to shape a country and a Europe that puts poverty eradication at the heart of its external relations.

2005: A Watershed for Irish Development Policy

Ireland has a strong and recognised tradition in overseas development. Connections with developing countries have extended in many directions and over many years. Rooted in a missionary past, these threads draw together tens of thousands of missionaries and volunteers; recognised ambassadors such as Mary Robinson, Bob Geldof and Bono; aid agencies and government programmes. This public face of Ireland is itself sustained by the private support of its citizens. Ireland is seen the world over as 'a caring country', due in no small part to this rich history.

Set against that history, 2005 was a remarkable year. From the enormous outpouring of generosity and support following the tsunami in south-east Asia in late December 2004, to the tens of thousands of people who came onto the streets of Dublin in June calling on the government to play its part in the drive to 'make poverty history', the spirit of volunteerism and the calls for political leadership on issues of aid, trade and debt show that 'caring' extends beyond 'charity'.[3]

The desire for a more just and equal world is also shown in our commitment to achieving the Millennium Development Goals.[4] As part of that commitment, the government promised in 2005 to reach the UN target of giving 0.7 per cent of GNI to Overseas Development Assistance (ODA) by 2012, three years ahead of the European target of 2015.

The year 2005 was notable too in that it marked the beginning of consultations on a White Paper on Official Development Assistance, which will be presented in 2006. This is the moment to carve out a strong and distinct role for Irish development policy. It is also the means by which political will and ambition across government and political parties can be realised.

The Irish government's overseas development programme, managed by Irish Aid, already has a strong reputation internationally. The White Paper is the opportunity to place poverty elimination within a coherent national policy framework that goes beyond Irish Aid and the Department of Foreign Affairs. This is a chance for government – on behalf of its citizens – to be bold and ambitious as never before.

Choices and Priorities

As our commitment to 0.7 per cent development aid is realised, there will be increasing focus on the quality and the value for money of the Irish government's aid programme. With increased resources, choices will have to be made. Should the programme expand into new countries, or should significantly more resources be given to a selected few countries? In these discussions, the question of competence will arise. What is Ireland good at? What added value does it bring? How does it make a distinctive impact on poverty eradication?

To answer these questions, and to realise a distinct role for Ireland among international donors, we should seek to offer something special and unique. Ireland should be seen as a world-class donor both in terms of the quantity of aid we deliver and the poverty focus of that aid. Indeed, Irish Aid should go further and position Ireland as a world leader in particular areas of emergency and development work.

Based on its history and experiences, as well as its current competencies and resource-base, Ireland could show leadership in a range of areas – including hunger (particularly in emergencies), conflict resolution and peace building, HIV/AIDS, and information and communication technology for development. In some of these areas, Ireland is already excelling; in others, it now has the opportunity to draw on its indigenous expertise (for example in R&D, pharmaceuticals and technology) and its grassroots support through volunteerism and mobilisation of citizens.

To become a world leader, we must first become world-class. We must define and master best practice and engage in a process of continuous improvement. This will require, above all, strong leadership at political, strategic and operational levels. It will also demand solid political commitment across government and a clear and significant investment plan.

As part of this plan, Irish Aid could help develop Irish partners who have the potential themselves to become world class in particular areas of expertise and operational capability and to add significantly to Irish Aid's own capability. This could involve NGOs, research and development institutions, academia, other arms of government and the private sector.

Ireland can play a leading role through strong positive influence and example-setting at EU and international levels. The forthcoming White Paper on Development Assistance should be the means by which citizens and government together can show meaningful commitment to building a better world for all.

A European Tradition of Development

The historical links between Ireland, Europe, Africa and other developing nations are as strong as they are diverse. As well as being the main trading partner for many developing countries, Europe is also home to thirty million migrants from Africa, Asia and Latin America.

The EU is also the largest donor in the world, playing a major role in overseas development. Its resources affect the lives of millions of people inside the Union but perhaps even greater numbers beyond its borders. The European Development Fund, to which EU Member States make voluntary contributions, has a potential spending power of €13.5 billion over the period 2001 to 2007.

The 2005 review of progress towards the Millennium Development Goals reaffirmed the contributions, efforts and activities of the EU and its Member States in support of these goals (Commission of the European Communities, 2005). These commitments reflect something of both the history of conflict out of which Europe emerged, and the shared values on which this community is based: democracy, equality, solidarity, social justice, human rights, tolerance and the international rule of law.

Distinct from any other international actor, Europe has moved towards political security through collective action, ever-closer cooperation, expansion of areas of self-interest and common policies towards economic prosperity, political growth and regional stability. Indeed, it is in this context that Ireland has flourished.

2005: A Watershed for European Development Policy

Paradoxically, in a year of internal dissonance on many issues, 2005 saw strong and united support from the European Union in the area of overseas development. Its commitments agreed at the June meeting of the European Council in advance of the UN Summit of September 2005 are worthy of particular note (Council of the European Union, 2005). When the assessment is made of 2005's global commitments to 'making poverty history', an important part of the story will be the strong promises made by Europe, promises which now must be honoured. In this respect, Ireland can provide vital leadership by delivering on the promises it has made and encouraging other Member States to do the same.

A further significant development was the signing by the Presidents of the European Council, the Commission and the Parliament of *The European Consensus on Development*, on 20 December 2005. This agreement 'provides, for the first time, a common vision that guides the action of the EU, both at its Members States and Community levels, in development cooperation'. Accompanying the Consensus is a statement of European Community Development Policy to guide implementation of the vision at Community level (European Parliament, Council, Commission, 2005, p. 3).

Europe has given expression to its core values through a Constitutional Treaty, and is giving meaning to these values through significant institutional reform. Whatever the fate of the current draft, the principles and provisions set out in the Constitution will be at the heart of debate on Europe in the coming years. Europe's foreign, security and defence policies will also continue apace. As this happens, ensuring that strong political priority is given to European Development Cooperation will become ever more challenging. How security and development policies evolve is of crucial significance, particularly for Africa.

The terrorist attacks in Madrid in 2004 brought the security agenda and its related priorities more sharply into focus. It prompted a clear commitment on the part of the EU Member States to work together to eliminate the root causes of terrorism. Poverty and injustice are two of most pervasive and challenging of these root causes, and an honest political commitment to countering terrorism can only be effective alongside a substantive political commitment to countering poverty and injustice.

EU foreign policy must be in the first instance values-based, and in the final analysis strategic and effective. It must therefore recognise that development is a prerequisite for peace and security. Ireland can and should reinforce this message at European level at every opportunity.

Unity in Diversity

There is another reason why Europe should show leadership in the fight against poverty. Development is one issue around which citizens unite. It is an area where both ambition and action have the clear support of Europe's large and diverse populations. It is also considered one of the elements that has contributed to the success of the EU.

As Europe grows, and develops its 'hard security' competencies, this must not detract from or undermine those core competencies it has developed over many years. In particular, Europe's development policy and its implementation must continue to be rooted in shared positive values. Public support for this position is reflected in a recent and sharp increase in the proportion of European citizens who believe it is important to help people in developing countries (Eurobarometer, 2005, p. 25). Ireland is well placed to deliver this message and reinforce this belief. Development is something we see as central to our own identity.

Finding our Voice

If we are to deliver this message, there must also be space for discussion and debate. During this 'period of reflection', a great deal has been said about the importance of 'engaging citizens' in the debate on Europe. The results of the *Eurobarometer 63*, the survey of public opinion carried out in May to June 2005, highlight just how necessary it is to bring European citizens and the European institutions closer together (Eurobarometer, 2005a). In an enlarged EU, with a growing number of civil society groups and organisations, this is a challenge, and it is one that should be set against another reality.

The experience of many in the development sector is that, contrary to the rhetoric, the space for civil society engagement is actually contracting. The practical difficulties in accessing support from and engagement with EU institutions run contrary to stated objectives of citizen engagement. In Ireland, the 'barriers to entry' are particularly high for small NGOs. Looking more broadly across the EU, civil society in new Member States is faced with significant difficulties in its engagement with European institutions.

Only a small number of NGOs in Ireland have the capacity to involve themselves meaningfully in the debates that shape European policy. Promoting interest in the European agenda among NGOs is difficult. All too often, the development agenda of the Union is seen as too complex, too distant and even irrelevant. The irony is that the policies of the EU fundamentally shape the day-to-day work of these NGOs. A further irony is that such engagement could, in fact, serve to strengthen support for the European project in all its dimensions.

The lives of millions of people in the developing world depend on public and political commitment to poverty eradication. To foster this commitment, civil society must be supported. National governments and European institutions have a central role in this regard. Resources must be available to help organisations become involved and develop their expertise. New impetus must be given to strengthening civil society and building capacity so that true engagement, debate and dialogue in relation to Europe's future and its efforts to eliminate poverty in that future are possible.

Now is the Time

As Ireland deals with the challenges of economic success and seeks to retain its traditional values in the context of a changing society, there is no greater contribution the country can make than to mobilise public intent and harness political capacity to set development as the area of highest priority for itself and for the EU. We should not underestimate the capacity of Ireland to play a key role in shaping the EU's policies on development on the back of our own proud record and firm commitments in this area.[5]

If we are to play this role, and at the same time increase understanding and support for the European project, we need a strong, vibrant and engaged civil society. We need public interest, policy expertise, creative communication strategies and increased capacity in all of these areas.

As a nation, we are increasingly confident, informed and outward-looking. There has never been a better time to promote public debate and focus political priority on the challenge of poverty eradication and our role as Irish and European citizens in meeting that challenge.

To again quote John F. Kennedy:

> Great powers have their responsibilities and their burdens, but the smaller nations of the world must fulfil their obligations as well. A great Irish poet once wrote: 'I believe profoundly in the future of Ireland, that this is an isle of destiny, that that destiny will be glorious, and that when our hour has come we will have something to give the world.'

Notes

1. Since 1973, Ireland has received from the EU at least 30 billion in agricultural support, 12 billion to upgrade infrastructure and 5 billion for spending on training and educating.
2. For three consecutive years, 2002 to 2004, Ireland was ranked by the Foreign Policy Globalisation Index as 'the most global nation in the world'. In 2005, it was ranked second to Singapore. This survey considers economic integration, technological connectivity, personal contact and political engagement. (www.atkearney.com)
3. 'The fact that we have people out on the street in Dublin today, demanding that we show leadership on this issue [overseas aid], is an encouraging signal that Europe is indeed big enough to look outwards, even during a period of introspection.' (José Manuel Barosso, President of the European Commission, Dublin, June 2005)
4. The eight Millennium Development Goals (MDGs) – which range from halving extreme poverty to halting the spread of HIV/AIDS and providing universal primary education, all by the target date of 2015 – form a blueprint agreed to by all the world's countries and all the world's leading development institutions. (http://www.un.org/millenniumgoals)
5. Dermot Ahern, TD, Minister for Foreign Affairs, National Forum on Europe, 20 October 2005.

References

Commission of the European Communities (2005) *EU Report on Millennium Development Goals 2000–2004: EU Contribution to the Review of the MDGs at the UN 2005 High Level Event*, Brussels:

Directorate-General Development.

Council of the European Union (2005) *Brussels European Council, 16 and 17 June 2005, Presidency Conclusions*, Brussels, 15.7.2005 (10255/1/05 REV 1).

Eurobarometer (2005) *Attitudes Towards Development Aid*, Special Eurobarometer. (http://europa.eu.int/comm/public_opinion/archives /ebs/ebs_222_en.pdf)

Eurobarometer (2005a) *Eurobarometer 63: Public Opinion in the European Union*. (http://europa.eu.int/comm/public_opinion/archives/eb/eb63/e b63en.pdf)

European Parliament, Council, Commission (2005) *The European Consensus on Development*, Joint Statement by the Council and the Representatives of the Governments of the Member States Meeting within the Council, the European Parliament and the Commission, 20.12.2005, *Official Journal of the European Union*, 24.2.2006 (2006/C 46/01).

The Opportunities and Challenges of Migration

Promoting a Comprehensive Agenda

Peter Bosch, Jean-Pierre Bou and Emma Haddad

Pressures at the Borders

Ceuta and Melilla, two Spanish cities on the North African Mediterranean coast, are nowadays surrounded by barbed-wire fences, intended to deter migrants from entering. And there are many migrants. They flee poverty and conflict across west and central Africa. They see Ceuta and Melilla as the gateway to Spain and Europe. For them, crossing these highly controlled borders is the best chance of reaching the European Union: the alternative is an even more hazardous sea crossing. At the end of September and beginning of October 2005, in the course of just five days, there was a series of mass attempts to enter these cities. At one point, around 700 people charged against two razor-wire security fences, with 200 to 300 managing to get over the border after the fence collapsed. A number of migrants lost their lives during their attempts to cross the border. These attempts were not isolated: in 2005 alone, more than 12,000 individuals attempted to enter Melilla in the hope of getting into Spain, and many others tried to reach Ceuta.

At first glance, the events that occurred in Ceuta and Melilla can be seen as a tragic one-off incident. Illegal migration from sub-Saharan Africa has risen sharply in recent years, and pressure on the borders had built up to such a degree by September 2005 that some kind of catastrophe was unavoidable. However, placing these events in their wider context can highlight a bigger picture – that of individuals feeling that their only course of action is to climb barbed-wired fences in a desperate attempt to reach European territory. In fact, what we are witnessing are the terrible consequences of the deterioration in the situation in Africa and the growing disparities between developed and developing countries. Most migrants are very much aware of the serious risks involved in attempting to make these journeys, yet staying in their country of origin is not seen as an option. The border between Morocco and Spain is just one of the places where the 'third' world quite literally meets the 'first'.

This article deals with the main factors behind these desperate attempts and the way the international community, and in particular the European Union, is trying to formulate a response. For reasons of space, the article cannot deal in much detail with the fundamental problems that contribute to the increase in international migration, but will focus instead on the EU policies and specific measures related directly to migration.

Push and Pull Factors in Migration

People have always moved and people will continue to move. For centuries Europe was a region of substantial emigration.[1] Today, the EU is a destination region for many migrants from all over the world and especially from developing countries. From 1990 to 2000 immigration accounted for 89 per cent of population growth in Europe. Migration is a reality – it will not go away. With globalisation, the volume and scale of migration, both internal and international, have increased, and look set to continue to do so, with the main movements being from developing to developed countries.[2]

The Global Commission on International Migration (2005) has stated:

> The number of people seeking to migrate from one country and continent to another will increase in the years to come, due to developmental and demographic disparities, as well as differences in the quality of governance. (p. 12)

If we apply the Commission's analysis to the African continent the following picture emerges. Demographically, Africa is growing quickly. In 1950, Africa had a population of 221 million, representing 8.7 per cent of the world's population; that figure now stands at 800 million or 13.5 per cent of world population. According to projections, population figures in Africa will reach 1.3 billion in 2025 and 1.75 billion in 2050. Meanwhile, economic growth has not matched demographic growth, so that hundreds of millions of Africans live in poverty. In 2001, 46.4 per cent of the sub-Saharan population lived on less than US$1 per day. Despite all the efforts of the international community, the gap in living standards between richer and poorer parts of the world is continuing to grow.[3]

The state of the labour market in developing countries also impacts on migratory movements. In many developing countries, market-oriented reforms have boosted the competitiveness of the national economy, but have failed to create sufficient jobs to absorb the growing number of people in the labour market, especially those without education and training. As a result, many young people are faced with the prospect of long-term unemployment or under-employment. At the same time, Africa is confronted by large-scale environmental degradation, which causes many people to leave their homes. Unexpected events such as the locust invasion in the Sahel region in 2003 will most likely continue to force people to seek refuge outside their countries of origin. In addition, disparities in the areas of democracy, governance, human rights and human security also contribute to international migration. There are still many African countries where the democratic process is fragile, where the rule of law is weak and where public administration is inefficient.

Poverty, fear and continued conflict on the African continent push people to search for a better life in more stable and developed regions, and Europe is often top of the list. At the same time, internal migration within Africa is taking place on a large scale: 50 per cent of the world's internally displaced persons and 28 per cent of the world's refugees are in Africa. There is, in addition, extensive labour migration between different countries and regions within Africa, particularly rural to urban migration. All of this means, of course, that in the medium term, migration pressure will increase yet further and the EU in particular will be exposed to it.

Coupled with these structural factors, border control of course plays a role. The European Union has strengthened its external border via efficient cooperation between EU Member States and their neighbours. At the Spanish–Moroccan border, police from the two authorities work side by side. Technology and repatriation agreements help stem the flow of illegal immigration and reaching the EU by sea is increasingly difficult. Yet the result of such cooperation at the border is that places such as Ceuta and Melilla represent the last opportunities to reach Europe. And the tight controls create a good market for traffickers, something many African countries simply cannot tackle adequately, notably because of lack of adequate resources.

Finally, the EU often provides a strong 'pull factor' for potential immigrants. Europe has the image of a place of opportunity. In fact, all industrialised countries need additional labour, especially cheap and flexible labour. As long as that demand is present, migrants will fill the gaps legally and illegally, often taking the jobs that citizens will not do. At the same time, historical links attract migrants to different areas of Europe. Many have networks of relatives and friends who can help them when they first arrive. Cultural ties and language are yet another pull factor.

A combination of all these factors can be seen to have played a part in the events that occurred in Ceuta and Melilla. Of the 17,252 foreign illegal immigrants apprehended in Morocco in 2004, 90 per cent were migrants from sub-Saharan Africa (Commission of the European Communities, 2005, p. 6). They also explain the arrivals of illegal migrants on the southern shores of the EU and why many people take the chance to make such a journey, often using the services of smuggling or trafficking gangs.

The European Policy Response

In a globalising world in which states, societies, economies and cultures are increasingly integrated and interdependent, international partnership becomes a necessity in an effort to manage the movement of people effectively. The real challenge for the international policy arena is to find ways for migration to bring real benefits to the countries concerned as well as to the migrants themselves, maximising these benefits while at the same time avoiding the potential risks, and ensuring that when an individual migrates he or she does so out of choice and through safe and legal means. Those are the key challenges policy-makers are confronted with today and to which answers need to be found urgently.

In the wake of the incidents in Ceuta and Melilla, migration rose straight back up to the top of the European agenda. It confirmed the EU in its view that addressing the challenges of international migration, especially from Africa, is a top priority. When European Heads of State and Government met informally in London on 27–28 October 2005, they agreed that Europe needs to do more to stop this kind of migration – the kind where individuals feel that their only option is to put themselves in the hands of traffickers or smugglers and climb walls and fences. They recognised that insufficiently managed migration flows can result in humanitarian disasters, be they deaths at sea, in the desert or in the back of lorries.

The EU approach to the external dimensions of migration policy is one of a spirit of partnership, seeking to promote a comprehensive agenda that reflects the full range of interests, priorities and anxieties of all countries concerned. Dialogue can therefore cover a variety of issues – from improvements in the management of legal migration flows and joint efforts to fight illegal immigration and human trafficking, to integration and rights of legal migrants and the strengthening of the linkages between migration and development. EU Heads of State and Government emphasised that responses to migration needed to be undertaken in partnership with all countries concerned – source, transit and destination. They emphasised too that respect for international obligations regarding human rights and the protection of vulnerable groups of people must be the basis for such policy responses.[4]

The European Commission took up the challenge to develop the comprehensive policy requested and subsequently issued *Priority Actions for Responding to the Challenges of Migration* on 30 November 2005 (Commission of the European Communities, 2005a). This document set out a series of immediate, practical actions to be taken forward in partnership with source and transit countries with a strong focus on north Africa and sub-Saharan countries.

Building on the Commission's Communication, European Member States identified a series of concrete measures and at the meeting of the European Council on 15–16 December 2005 they adopted the policy statement, *Global Approach to Migration: Priority Actions Focusing on Africa and the Mediterranean* (Council of the European Union, 2005). This constitutes an ambitious agenda, with action envisaged in three areas: strengthening cooperation and action between Member States; working with key countries of origin in Africa and working with neighbouring countries in the Mediterranean region. The actions will be implemented over the course of 2006 by the Commission, Member States, bodies such as FRONTEX (the borders security agency of the EU) and international organisations, all working closely together.

The list of priority actions is extensive: expressing the will to work in partnership, the EU will engage with African countries on migration issues in a comprehensive and structured manner. Ministers from EU Member States will meet their counterparts in north and sub-Saharan African countries in an EU–Africa regional conference, bringing together source, transit and destination countries to talk about migration issues of common interest and concern for the first time. Comprehensive dialogue and action will be stepped up with the African Union, the main regional organisation representing African states. Dialogue will be initiated with key sub-Saharan African countries on a bilateral basis, dealing with a range of issues such as legal migration; workers' rights; fair treatment and integration; anti-discrimination; illegal migration and smuggling and trafficking in human beings; readmission of illegal migrants. The EU will offer assistance to African countries to allow them to build capacity to better manage their own migration systems. 'Migration profiles' will be developed as a tool to help bring together all the information required to develop and implement a national migration strategy.

European and African states may also work together to support the development of African states' asylum systems to provide better protection to refugees and more effective assistance to countries faced with mass influxes of refugees or large-scale internal displacement. The

EU will reinforce its responsibilities for enhancing protection for refugees and international protection outside the EU, with a pilot regional protection programme being launched, focusing on Tanzania and the surrounding countries. At the same time, the EU will offer to support African counties in meeting their obligations under the Convention Governing the Specific Aspects of Refugee Problems in Africa, which was adopted by Heads of African States and Government in 1969.

EU Member States will also reinforce their cooperation in the Mediterranean. Joint operations and pilot projects will be initiated in 2006 and a feasibility study on a surveillance system for the southern maritime borders of the EU will be launched. A risk analysis report on Africa will be completed, identifying the most important routes taken by migrants who cross the continent on dangerous and illegal journeys, and an analysis of the gaps in international legislation of the sea will be carried out. The EU will also seek to support Member States in times of mass influx of persons at their borders. To that end, a proposal for rapid reaction teams made up of national experts from the different Member States will be formulated. The Commission has indicated it will allocate up to 3 per cent of the relevant Community financial programmes for migration issues.

These priority actions will be part of a wider EU policy on migration in which the fight against illegal immigration and human trafficking and the promotion of a EU policy on legal migration will be key components. Although it is clear that the EU needs immigration, not least to face the challenge of ageing populations, there is a common understanding that such immigration must happen in an orderly and managed way. In this respect, EU Member States, like all countries, obviously have a right to control access to and stay on their territories. The Commission will shortly issue a Communication that will propose concrete measures for stepping up action in the fight against illegal immigration in key areas, such as document security and illegal working.

The fight against human trafficking is another important priority. In October 2005, the Commission issued a Communication, *Fighting Trafficking in Human Beings: An Integrated Approach and Proposals for an*

Action Plan (Commission of the European Communities, 2005b). This aims at further strengthening the commitment of the EU and Member States to prevent and fight trafficking in human beings for reasons of sexual or labour exploitation, and to help protect, support and rehabilitate its victims. It underlines that the needs and rights of the persons concerned must be at the centre of any EU policy against human trafficking.[5] This means first and foremost a clear commitment by the EU institutions and Member States to follow a human rights-centred approach and to promote it in their external relations and development policies.[6]

In the domain of legal migration, a number of important positive steps towards a real EU immigration policy have already been taken, including adoption of directives on admission of third-country nationals for study and training and to carry out scientific research (Council of the European Union, 2004 and 2005a). The EU needs migration, but in order to meet its labour needs it needs the right migrants.[7] As long as the EU and its Member States are confronted with an inflow of people who do not match current needs of the EU labour market, they will not be able to compete effectively on an increasingly global labour market. The lack of socio-economic compatibility has serious consequences, both for the newly arrived and for our societies, as the possibilities for smooth integration are limited.

In December 2005, the Commission presented a *Policy Plan on Legal Migration* (Commission of the European Communities, 2005c), which in effect maps out the various initiatives that the EU will take in this area over the next four years, corresponding to the duration of 'The Hague Programme' (see Council of the European Union, 2004a). The Policy Plan covers four main areas of activity: legislative initiatives relating to the admission of economic migrants; initiatives to improve the gathering and the dissemination of information and of data on the various aspects of migratory phenomena; measures and policies in relation to the integration of third-country nationals; measures that will be developed in cooperation with countries of origin. On the latter, it is notable that the Commission is proposing the possibility for former migrants to obtain a residence permit for temporary employment in the former host country. The Commission would also like to encourage the growth of professional and linguistic courses in countries of origin.

Migration and Development: The Need to Think Long-Term

While the priority actions agreed in December 2005 constitute the immediate focus, there is a need to address also longer-term issues and in particular to explore in greater detail the relationship between migration policy and development policy. In September 2005, the Commission issued a Communication, *Migration and Development: Some Concrete Orientations*, which looks specifically at how well-designed policies can help enhance the positive impact of migration on development (Commission of the European Communities, 2005d). Focused on migration from developing countries to the EU, the Communication addresses four sets of issues: migrants' remittances; the role of diasporas as actors in home country development; return migration and the transfer of skills; and efforts to curb 'brain drain'. In each, it seeks to define 'concrete orientations' for improving the linkages between migration and development. Moreover, by helping to create more opportunities in countries of origin, these orientations should also contribute, in the medium term, to mitigating push factors in these countries.

The Communication contains many recommendations for future action. In relation to remittances, it states that efforts must be made, in conjunction with other institutions such as the World Bank, to improve our knowledge of migrant remittance flows (money sent back by migrants to their countries of origin). The Global Commission on International Migration (2005) noted that while accurate figures in relation to remittances are hard to obtain, the World Bank had estimated the annual value of formally transferred remittances in 2004 to be $150 billion, representing a 50 per cent increase in just five years and almost three times the value of Official Development Assistance (p. 26). While recognising that remittances are private money, the European Commission is exploring ways to make the procedures for sending this money more efficient and reliable and is considering how these money flows could be better used to achieve development goals. Noting that diasporas 'are increasingly recognised as an important potential actor in the development of countries of origin' (p. 6), the Communication says that the Commission is looking at ways to help interested developing countries reach out to and maintain links with their diasporas, as well as exploring the issue of engaging diaspora organisations in the policy-development process.

The Communication also considers the role of return migration in enabling migrants to share the skills and expertise they have acquired in their countries of residence with their countries of origin. Return can take various forms, from permanent return to temporary return through the various forms of 'circular migration', by which migrants go back and forth between their countries of origin and residence. Such forms of mobility, which are regarded as highly beneficial in terms of transfer of skills and knowledge, can be facilitated by appropriate policies – for example, policies to ensure the portability of pension rights and other entitlements for returning migrants, to foster the recognition of qualifications obtained elsewhere or to ensure that migrants willing to participate in temporary return schemes will not lose their residence rights in the country of destination.

Finally, the increasing labour needs of industrialised countries have the potential to impact extremely negatively on the development capacity of developing countries. The example of 'brain drain' in the health sector is well known. The shortage of nurses in most of the industrialised world is expected to increase sharply in the coming years with ageing populations across Europe needing medical attention and enrolment in nursing schools declining.[8] In 1999, Ghana's losses to emigration included 320 nurses – the same number of nurses who qualify in the country each year; twice as many were lost in the following year. In Kenya, health clinics have closed and many others are severely understaffed due to a lack of adequate personnel. At the same time, sub-Saharan low-income countries will need to double their health care workforces in the coming years, recruiting at least 620,000 nurses to be able to tackle their severe health emergencies (Chen et al, 2004).

These are just some examples highlighting why the EU will be actively involved in the debate about how to ensure that our migration policies do not lead to brain drain, as emphasised in the Commission Communication, *EU Strategy for Action on the Crisis in Human Resources for Health in Developing Countries* (Commission of the European Communities, 2005e). This Communication recommends restraints on active recruitment of health care professionals from the developing world and cooperation with the WHO on these issues and also looks at how EU financial assistance can help developing countries address skills shortages in this key area.

It is this longer-term approach that must go hand-in-hand with any action taken in the short term. Creating jobs and livelihoods in low-income countries will have a significant impact on migration and such a development can only be successful if and when countries of origin and destination are ready to share rights and responsibilities in a joint effort.

Trade policies will also have to play an important role in promoting development, alleviating poverty and creating sustainable livelihoods. Participants in the Doha round of World Trade Organisation negotiations should seek to maximise the welfare gains generated by the multilateral trading system and find ways of attributing these gains in a fair and balanced manner. Assuming real responsibility for the welfare of their citizens and creating the conditions in which people are able to meet their needs, exercise their human rights and realise their potential and fulfil their aspirations also needs to be part of the approach.

When it comes to Africa, the EU is active on all these fronts. Adopted at the end of 2005, *The EU and Africa: Towards a Strategic Partnership* sets out the steps that the EU will take with Africa between now and 2015 to support African efforts to build a peaceful, democratic and prosperous future for all its peoples, with the primary aim of achieving the Millennium Development Goals and the promotion of sustainable development, security and good governance in Africa (Council of the European Union, 2005b). On migration specifically, the strategy states the intention to:

> Maximise the developmental benefits and minimize the negative aspects of migration and strengthen protection for refugees, through engaging in balanced dialogue and cooperation with the AU [African Union], other African organisations and states on a broad range of migration issues. (p. 6)

The document notes that the core principles of the strategy are partnership based on international law and human rights, equality and mutual accountability with the underlying philosophy being African ownership and responsibility, including working through African institutions. Promoting respect of human rights and good governance will be of central importance. The recent decision of the World Bank to put loans on hold for a number of countries that did not meet the basic standards should be seen as an encouraging sign. It is to be hoped that new and emerging global economic players will follow the traditions of the EU to systematically ensure that respect for human rights is part of their relationship with developing countries.

Conclusion

International migration will continue to pose serious challenges and opportunities for our societies in the years to come. Provided it is well managed and that all actors fulfil their responsibilities, it can have a beneficial effect. The EU and its Member States will need to act collectively to meet their obligations to develop and implement a comprehensive policy approach in close cooperation with partner countries and international organisations. Without such an approach and the determination to make it a success, we will be simply waiting for another Ceuta and Melilla to happen.

Notes

1. Between 1830 and 1930 around 60 million Europeans emigrated, many heading for the USA and Canada. After the Second World War another five million left.

2. From 1980 to 2000, the number of migrants living in the developed world increased from 48 to 110 million, compared with an increase from 52 to 65 million in the developing world.

3. Gross Domestic Product in high-income countries was 41 times greater than that of middle-income countries in 1975: it is now 61 times greater (see Global Commission on International Migration, 2005, p. 12). Taking one specific example: in 1975 the income gap between Spain and Morocco was around 1:4; today, it is around 1:14.

4. The current overall framework for EU migration and asylum policy is provided by 'The Hague Programme', an ambitious five-year work programme adopted by European Heads of State and Government in November 2004 (Council of the European Union 2004a). It has a strong emphasis on immigration and the need to develop the external side of migration and asylum policies of the EU.

5. Work on fighting trafficking at the EU level is in line with the United Nations Convention Against Organised Crime and its Protocol to prevent, suppress and punish trafficking in persons. (http://www.unodc.org/unodc/crime_cicp_convention.html)

6. Respect for human rights is a central element in the Commission's approach to migration. In 2007, the Commission will submit a proposal for a directive on the rights that third-country workers will be able to enjoy once admitted to the territory of a Member State, even before they become long-term residents, with the aim of establishing comparable conditions throughout the Union for all migrant workers in a regular situation.

7. 'Out of a total of 720,000 Med-MENA [Mediterranean countries of the Middle East and North Africa] first-generation migrants with a university degree, 392,000, i.e. 54%, are residing in Canada and the USA alone, while 87% of those who have a lower than primary, a primary or a secondary level of education are in Europe.' (Fargues, 2005, p. 21)

8. A number of EU Member States look to developing countries for the direct recruitment of medical staff. The United Kingdom, for example, has relied on nurses coming from African countries such as Botswana, Ghana, Kenya, Malawi, Nigeria, South Africa, Zambia and Zimbabwe – all former British colonies – many of which have been among those hit

hardest by the HIV pandemic. (See Chagututu and Vallebhaneni, 2005) It should be noted, however, that the UK has a Code of Conduct for ethical recruitment in the health sector. It is not only in the EU that there are shortages of health sector personnel: 126,000 nursing positions are currently unfilled in US hospitals.

References

Chaguturu, Sreekanth and Snigdha Vallabhaneni (2005) 'Aiding and Abetting – Nursing Crises at Home and Abroad', *The New England Journal of Medicine*, Vol. 353, No. 17 (27 October 2005), pp. 1761–3.

Chen, Lincoln et al. (2004) 'Human Resources for Health: Overcoming the Crisis', *The Lancet*, No. 364, pp. 1984–90.

Commission of the European Communities (2005) *Mission Report*, Technical Mission to Morocco; Visit to Ceuta and Melilla on Illegal Immigration, 7–11 October 2005.

Commission of the European Communities (2005a) *Priority Actions for Responding to the Challenges of Migration: First Follow-up to Hampton Court*, Communication from the Commission to the Council and the European Parliament, Brussels, 30.11.2005, COM (2005) 621 final.

Commission of the European Communities (2005b) *Fighting Trafficking in Human Beings – An Integrated Approach and Proposals for an Action Plan*, Communication from the Commission to the European Parliament and Council, Brussels, 18.10 2005, COM (2005) 514 final.

Commission of the European Communities (2005c) *Policy Plan on Legal Migration*, Communication from the Commission, Brussels, 21.12.2005, COM (2005) 669 final.

Commission of the European Communities (2005d) *Migration and Development: Some Concrete Orientations*, Communication from the Commission to the Council, the European Parliament, the European Economic and Social Committee and the Committee of the Regions, Brussels, 1.9.2005, COM (2005) 390 final.

Commission of the European Communities (2005e) *EU Strategy for Action on the Crisis in Human Resources for Health in Developing Countries*, Communication from the Commission to the Council and the European Parliament, Brussels, 12.12.2005, COM (2005) 642 final.

Council of the European Union (2004) *Directive on the Conditions of Admission of Third-Country Nationals for the Purposes of Studies, Pupil Exchange, Unremunerated Training or Voluntary Service*, Council Directive

2004/114/EC of 13 December 2004, *Official Journal of the European Union*, L 375, 23.12.2004, pp. 12–18.

Council of the European Union (2004a) 'The Hague Programme: Strengthening Freedom, Security and Justice in the European Union' in *Presidency Conclusions, Brussels European Council, 4/5 November 2004*, Brussels, 8 December 2004, 14292/1/04, Annex 1.

Council of the European Union (2005) 'Global Approach to Migration: Priority Actions Focussing on Africa and the Mediterranean' in *Presidency Conclusions, Brussels European Council, 15/16 December 2005*, Brussels, 30 January 2006, 15914/1/05, Annex 1.

Council of the European Union (2005a) *Directive on Specific Procedures for Admitting Third-Country Nationals to Carry out Scientific Research*, Council Directive 2005/71/EC of 12 October 2005, *Official Journal of the European Union*, L 289, 3.11.2005, pp. 15–22.

Council of the European Union (2005b) *The EU and Africa: Towards a Strategic Partnership*, Brussels, 19 December 2005, 15961/05 (Presse 367).

Fargues, Philippe (2005) (ed.) *Mediterranean Migration – 2005 Report* (Cooperation project on the social integration of immigrants, migrants, and the movement of persons, financed by the European Commission MEDA Programme), Florence: EUI–RSCAS, CARIM Consortium. (www.carim.org)

Global Commission on International Migration (2005) *Migration in an Interconnected World: New Directions for Action*, Geneva: Global Commission on International Migration. (www.gcim.org)

The views expressed in this article are those of the authors and do not bind the European Commission.

Migration in Europe

Fortress Europe or Opportunity Europe?[1]

Alan Dukes

A dictionary definition of 'migration' is 'the movement of persons from one country or locality to another'. For the European Union, migration can take several forms. It can mean the movement of persons from one Member State to another. It can mean the movement of persons into the EU from third countries and the movement of persons from the EU to third countries. It can mean the movement of persons from a third country into an EU Member State and from that Member State to another.

Each form of migration has potentially different consequences for the person moving, for the country or locality of origin and for the receiving country or locality.

These consequences can be complex. They can be, *inter alia*:

- Demographic (for example, population size, age profile, gender balance, fertility rates);
- Social (for example, ethnic diversity, cultural diversity, educational tradition);
- Economic (for example, employment and unemployment, requirements of social services, social infrastructure requirements).

The extent of the migration issue has been described by Jan O. Karlsson, Co-Chair of the Global Commission on International Migration:

> In the last 25 years, the number of international migrants more than doubled to some 200 million. While migrants are to be found in every part of the globe, with many of them moving from one developing country to another, most of the recent growth in migrant numbers has taken place in the industrialised states of

Europe, North America and the Asia-Pacific region. This trend seems certain to continue. (Karlsson, 2005)

Karlsson goes on to say: 'The EU, which for historical and geographical reasons has close connections with many developing countries, has been – and will continue to be – a prime destination for people who feel that they are unable to meet their needs, fulfil their aspirations and exercise their human rights in their country or region of origin.' (Karlsson, 2005)

Migration: Has it a Function or an Objective?

Why do people move from one country or locality to another? What purpose does migration serve? Is it, or can it be, directed or planned?

Our theme suggests that we are not concerned with the voluntary international movement of professional or skilled people in the course of their career development or simply in search of a more congenial place to live. We are concerned with the movement of people who are:

- In fear of political or social oppression, in fear of threats to their physical safety and security, or who are forced to leave their homes as a result of violence or war;
- Forced to move as a result of an ethnically based policy being pursued by a power group;
- Under economic pressure to find employment to support at least a minimum acceptable living for their families, where such opportunities are not available to them in their countries or localities of origin, or to find a better way of life than that available to them there.

The first and second categories are refugees, asylum seekers or displaced persons; the third are generally regarded as economic migrants.

The Global Commission on International Migration has described the driving forces of international migration as 'the three Ds': development, demography and democracy. (Karlsson, 2005)

The objective of economic migrants is typically permanent relocation. That is not necessarily the case for refugees, asylum seekers or displaced persons. On the face of it, it seems that while *immigration* can be prevented or limited, it cannot be planned or directed except, perhaps, in cases of agreed transfer of population. It appears that *emigration* can be planned, directed or influenced by powers that are ethnically motivated and prepared to use force or, in the case of agreed transfer of population, that it can be prevented or limited by law and by strict enforcement measures.

The objectives of receiving countries or localities (to the extent that it makes any sense to speak of objectives in this context) can clearly be quite different to those of migrants. Many receiving countries articulate their policies in relation to economic immigrants on the basis of perceived skill requirements or shortages. There are many examples, among which we might cite Australia, which has operated such a policy, and Ireland where policy in relation to non-EU immigrants is largely based on perceived skill shortages in the Irish labour force.

Migration in EU Member States

There is an extra dimension to migration in the EU Member States. Freedom of movement and of establishment for EU nationals are among the basic principles of the EU. This means that any citizen of any Member State is entitled to live, to work and to set up a business in any other Member State. In general, exceptions to this principle arise only in relation to freedom of establishment in professions or occupations which are subject to state recognition or authorisation and where there is no established system for the mutual recognition of qualifications. In principle, no discrimination may be applied to the conditions of entry into courses of study or qualification for such professions or occupations.

These principles are fully applied by the fifteen Member States which formed the EU up to 1 May 2004. On that date, ten new Member States joined the EU. Their Accession Treaties contain provisions derogating temporarily from the application of freedom of movement and of establishment. This allows the 'fifteen' not to grant the same freedom of movement and of establishment to citizens of the new Member States as they grant to citizens of the 'fifteen'. Ireland, the UK and Sweden opted not to apply those derogations but to allow full freedom of movement and of establishment.

In general, a person who is legitimately in an EU Member State has the right to move freely between Member States. This means that the right of that person to be in the EU and to travel freely between Member States must be established at the point of first arrival in the EU. In this sense, every Member State is at the external border of the EU. A person who is in any Member State of the EU without the requisite permissions can be refused passage from that Member State to any other.

All twenty-five EU Member States are bound by provisions made under the Geneva Conventions in relation to the treatment of refugees and asylum seekers. The nature, effectiveness and speed of administrative practices and procedures vary substantially from one Member State to another.

There is, as yet, no single, comprehensive body of EU law and practice covering the treatment of immigrants into the EU, perhaps because Member States regard immigration as a particularly sensitive subject. Nevertheless, considerable progress has been made in this direction.

- In November 2004, the Justice and Home Affairs Council adopted Common Basic Principles (CBPs) on the integration of third-country nationals (Council of the European Union, 2004).
- On 1 September 2005, the EU Commission published a *Common Agenda* for a framework for the integration of third-country nationals in the EU. This includes the announcement of the Commission's intention to set up a European Integration Forum involving the Member States and stakeholders such as EU umbrella organisations involved in integration (Commission of the European Communities, 2005);
- On 14 April 2005, the Justice and Home Affairs Council selected Warsaw as the location for FRONTEX, the European Agency for the Management of Operational Cooperation at the External Borders of the Member States of the European Union.

The absence of a single, harmonised body of law and practice has sometimes given rise to difficulties and disputes between Member States as to where responsibility lies for making decisions on applications for asylum. As a general rule, this lies with the Member State in which the applicant first makes entry to the EU. There have been suggestions (not to put it any more strongly) that certain Member States turned a blind eye to immigrants from third countries as long as they were in transit to another Member State. This practice may have given rise to certain favoured trafficking routes.

The fact that not all Member States adhere to the Schengen Agreement[2] is a further complicating factor. It is still the case, for example, that Ireland and the UK operate a common passport area. Following the UK decision to remain outside the Schengen area, Ireland decided to adopt the same approach so as not to disturb this arrangement. This was motivated by the fact that some 70 per cent of movements of persons into and out of Ireland are to or from the UK.

In recent years, the advantages of 'borderless' travel between EU Member States other than by surface transport have been substantially vitiated by security concerns. These now mean that air travellers are obliged to show some form of evidence of identity when leaving or entering a Member State.

So much for the mechanics of the system: what about the philosophy – if, indeed, there is one?

Fortress Europe or Opportunity Europe?

The notion of 'Fortress Europe' clearly suggests an unwelcoming environment, with strong defences in place to deny access to outsiders. Does that describe the European Union, either in the past or today? On the whole, I think not.

A number of Member States have large populations with ethnic roots elsewhere in the world. Starting in the north, we find Sweden, which has for many years been very open to receiving refugees from many parts of the world. Even though their numbers may be relatively small (perhaps because of the rigours of the Swedish winter), they are a group with influence far beyond the borders of their adoptive country. Denmark has had a similar tradition, although on a smaller scale. Germany has for many years had a very substantial Turkish population, almost all of them followers of Islam.

The Netherlands' population includes a great many people of east Indian origin and, in more recent years, people of north African origin. A great many, if not the majority, of these people are Muslims. France has a very large population of people from both north and west Africa, the majority of whom are followers of Islam. It has some significant groups who originated in the Caucasus. It is, perhaps, interesting to recall that France provided a haven for Russians, some of whom went there to escape the attentions of the Tsars and some who went to escape the attentions of the Bolsheviks.

The UK has perhaps the most diverse mix of non-European ethnic groups with, *inter alia*, people of Pakistani, Bangladeshi, Indian, South African, West Indian and Chinese origin. They include Muslims, Buddhists, Hindu, Taoist and Christians of diverse traditions. Spain has a very large population of north African origin, mainly Muslim. Italy has a substantial north African, mainly Muslim, population and, in recent years, an increasing number of people of Balkan origin. The new Member States have brought some new elements to the picture. The three Baltic States, and Latvia in particular, have significant population groups of Russian origin.

In Ireland, we have only recently begun to understand what it is to be a receiving country. In the last fifteen years, Ireland has gone from being a country of net emigration to being a country experiencing a substantial net inflow of population.

The first manifestation of this change came with the reversal, in the 1990s, of the Irish diaspora. Irish people who had made successful careers abroad began to return to Ireland to continue their careers. Data for the year up to April 2005 show that the numbers of returning Irish exceeded the numbers of Irish people emigrating: the former totalled 19,000, the latter 16,600 (Central Statistics Office, 2005, pp. 7–8). Irish people now go abroad not because they cannot find employment in Ireland, but because a spell in another country will be useful in their career development, or because they simply like the idea of spending some time abroad. Economic depression at home has long since ceased to be the impetus for emigration.

During that last fifteen years, economic growth and improved social provision have made Ireland a more apparently attractive destination for refugees and asylum-seekers. Conflicts in Africa and in the Balkans have added to the overall numbers of people seeking asylum and refuge. A growing taste for freedom, allied to greater knowledge of conditions of life in EU Member States, has contributed to a greater flow of people from former USSR countries now in the Commonwealth of Independent States (CIS) – for example, Belarus, Ukraine and Moldova. We can speculate also that difficulties experienced by applicants for asylum in other EU Member States contributed to flows towards Ireland. Traffickers and smugglers have added their contribution to the numbers of people crossing borders into the EU.

Ireland has accommodated 'programme refugees' from war zones (principally Kosovo). Most of these have now returned to their home areas. We have had a significant inflow from Africa, particularly from Nigeria. There are noticeable numbers of citizens from CIS countries among us. Only a few years ago, any Asians we saw on our streets were almost bound to be tourists. Today, Asian students and workers in all kinds of occupations are commonly to be seen.

In the year ending April 2005, 26,400 people are recorded as having entered Ireland from the new EU Member States alone. (Proportionately, this is the equivalent of about 350,000 people entering the UK, France or Germany.) A further 13,100 people entered from the other EU Member States, including the UK (proportionately equivalent to about 175,000 people entering the UK, France or Germany). Curiously, the number of people from the new EU Member States issued with PPS numbers in the same year was 84,000. Perhaps large numbers were already in Ireland before they became entitled to PPS numbers.

Data up to April 2005 show that the inflow to Ireland from countries other than EU Member States and the USA has been declining: in the year ending April 2002 the number of such immigrants stood at 21,700 but in the year ending April 2005 it had fallen to 9,000 (Central Statistics Office, 2005, p. 8).

Whatever we may say about the circumstances in which non-nationals arrive and live in our midst, we can hardly describe the EU as a 'fortress', closed to the outside world. It may be difficult to get through the gates, the accommodation inside may be frequently unsatisfactory, but it is not a closed fortress.

On the evidence before us, I think it more accurate to characterise the EU as a place of opportunity for immigrants than as a fortress. The quality of the opportunity offered may often be limited. The conditions of access to that opportunity may often be unequal or unfair. The motives for granting the opportunity may often reflect self-interest on the part of the receiving state, rather than an unambiguously humane concern. Notwithstanding all this, it seems to me that the EU is more a place of opportunity for third-country nationals than an unattainable goal or an inaccessible haven.

The Treatment of Migrants

Refugees, Asylum Seekers and Displaced Persons

As already pointed out, there is no single, comprehensive body of EU law and practice covering the treatment of immigrants from third countries, but a number of steps have been taken to coordinate national provisions. All the Member States are bound by UN provisions on the treatment of refugees and asylum seekers, but we should, from time to time, review the basis of these provisions and both the spirit and the context in which we apply them.

In general, the first step is to establish whether persons presenting themselves at the border are *bona fide* refugees or asylum seekers. Basically, this judgement has to do with the political situation in the applicant's country or region of origin. An assessment is made as to whether the applicant would be in danger of death, oppression or serious denial of rights if returned. There is frequently a suspicion (spoken or unspoken) that there is no such danger and that the applicant is, in fact, an economic migrant rather than a *bona fide* refugee. I have no doubt that 'correct' decisions are very frequently made, either to accept or to reject requests for asylum. Equally, I have no doubt that 'incorrect' decisions – in both directions – are not rare.

Whatever the motivation of a person's decision to leave his or her country or region of origin, the decision itself is bound to be traumatic. Nobody makes such a decision lightly. Is it, then, reasonable for the requested country to apply different treatments in response to different motivations? It is difficult to find a fully humane reason for such a distinction. Extreme poverty must often be as difficult to endure as political or physical oppression.

One reason for granting refugee status or for accepting a request for political asylum is the determination that the applicant would be put in physical danger of some serious kind if returned to the region or country of origin. Is extreme poverty not a form of serious danger – indeed, a potentially mortal danger?

In my view, we should be very conscious of the effect of severity in the application of criteria for admission. The more severe the tests and the more frequent the refusals, the greater the incentive to try to circumvent the system. There is a real and observed danger that severity in the application of entry tests acts as an incentive to trafficking, with all of the horrible consequences it so often entails.

Given the principle of freedom of movement within the EU (even if it is temporarily qualified in the case of citizens of the new Member States), there is a compelling case for identity of treatment of all refugees and asylum seekers by all of the EU Member States.

If we accept that there are legitimate reasons for refusing applications for refugee status or for asylum, the basic principles of the EU law, our adherence to UN principles and to the European Convention on Human Rights must oblige all Member States to provide common and respectful conditions for the maintenance of unsuccessful applicants pending their return to their countries of origin. The variety of practices among the Member States and the unsatisfactory provisions made by some have recently and rightly been the subject of some debate and controversy.

Economic Migrants

There is a logical case for proposing that one of the objectives in the EU's policies in regard to developing countries should be the removal of the incentive for economic migration. In other words, we should assist developing countries to move toward full employment. The more we succeed in this, the smaller will be the incentive to migrate. This is, of course, a utopian view.

For as long as there is an economic incentive to migrate, we are called upon to respond. The argument then concerns the conditions under which we accept economic migrants. As I have already pointed out, there are countries that see their approach to this issue as part of their labour market policy. There is a burgeoning literature on the articulation of immigration policy as an instrument to be used in offsetting the effects of the 'greying' of western European societies, with its implications for dependency ratios, the funding of pensions and so on.

Such an approach is, of course, entirely logical. It is also entirely self-interested. It constitutes nothing less than *dirigiste* social engineering of a kind which would hardly be accepted as part of a 'domestic' labour market policy. It treats migrant workers as economic cyphers. It is the basis of the approach which leads to work visas being issued to employers rather than to employees. It results in migrant workers being tied to a given employer for any kind of career development. It introduces a new form of rigidity into one part of the labour market. It can encourage 'shadow economy' practices, with serious dangers of exploitation of a new category of vulnerable workers. It clearly works against the full integration of migrant workers into the workforce. Inevitably, too, it militates against the integration of migrant workers and their families into their host societies.

Integration

There seems to be a general acceptance of the proposition that we should aim to facilitate the integration of immigrants into their host societies. The question of what we mean by 'integration' has always been a matter of some uncertainty. Since 7 July 2005, it has become an issue of heightened concern with the revelation that young people of immigrant origin born, educated, socialised and employed in the UK were prepared to participate in violent attacks against that society.

What do we mean by 'integration'? It seems to me that there would be general agreement on the proposition that 'integration' means that the receiving society should accord immigrants such things as:

- Equal rights to work;
- Equal access to social provisions of all kinds;
- The right to family unification;
- The right to education;
- Freedom of conscience, religion and speech;
- Full civil rights;
- The right to participate in civil society, in its broadest definition, on an equal footing with the indigenous population.

It seems to me also that there is a matching obligation on the part of the immigrant, the mirror image of the obligations of the receiving society, always provided that the immigrant has the same right as nationals of a country to choose the appropriate or desired level of active participation.

For the immigrant, 'integration' should mean:

- Acceptance of the constitutional foundation of the host society;
- Acceptance of the civil order;
- Recognition of the rights of fellow immigrants to choose freely their own levels of personal participation in the legitimate activities of civil society in all its manifestations;
- Respect for the social norms of the receiving society.

Observation of immigrant groups in EU Member States suggests that many of them have not experienced or achieved full integration in the terms in which I have suggested it should be defined. Integration is not a one-way street and failure to achieve it results from deficiencies on both sides. We need to develop a greater understanding of those deficiencies if we are to have any real prospect of finding remedies.

Conclusion

In the matter of immigration, today's EU is not a fortress. Neither is it a land of unlimited opportunity. An assessment of the response of the EU to inward migration shows, on balance, a postive outcome; however, we could still do much better.

Notes

1. This paper was presented at the conference, *The Future of Europe: Uniting Vision, Values and Citizens?*, held in Dublin on 27 September 2005.

2. The Shengen Agreement was concluded in June 1985 when seven European countries signed a treaty to end internal border controls and checkpoints, in effect delineating a territory without internal borders. Since then, eight more countries have signed the treaty, including two – Iceland and Norway – which are not in the European Union. Neither Ireland nor the UK is party to the Shengen Agreement. The fifteen Shengen countries are: Austria, Belgium, Denmark, Finland, France, Germany, Iceland, Italy, Greece, Luxembourg, The Netherlands, Norway, Portugal, Spain and Sweden.

References

Central Statistics Office (2005) *Population and Migration Estimates, April 2005,* Dublin: Central Statistics Office.

Commission of the European Communities (2005) *A Common Agenda for Integration: Framework for the Integration of Third-Country Nationals in the European Union,* Communication from the Commission to the Council, the European Parliament, the European Economic and Social Committee and the Committee of the Regions, Brussels, 1.9.2005, COM (2005) 389 final.

Council of the European Union (2004) *Press Release: 2618ᵗʰ Council Meeting, Justice and Home Affairs,* Brussels, 14615/04 (Presse 321).

Karlsson, Jan O. (2005) 'Development, Demography and Demcocracy: Driving Forces of International Migration', *Challenges to Europe Online Journal,* Issue 14 – *Towards a European Area of Freedom, Security and Justice?,* 16 September 2005.

The views expressed in this article are those of the author only; the Institute of European Affairs has not been consulted on them and bears no responsibility for them.

European Migration and Asylum Policy

The Challenge of Upholding Justice, Freedom and Solidarity[1]
Doris Peschke

In 1975, I participated in a school excursion to West Berlin. Of course, we visited the famous museums, but also the Berlin Wall. We saw a memorial to people who had died when they tried to cross the border from the East to the West. We also made a visit to East Berlin, crossing the border with passport checks and with the necessity of changing a restricted amount of money for the day.

At that time, we were taught that this fence was limiting the freedom of people – freedom of movement, freedom of thought and speech. We learned that people resisted these controls and demanded their human rights.

Today, when I hear of another boat sunk in the Mediterranean, with people drowned, or barely making it to Italy or Spain, or about another lorry found carrying people who had tried to cross into the EU but had died during the journey, or when I see the fences and watch towers at the Channel Tunnel, I am reminded of this first encounter with closed borders. And I ask myself: is freedom restricted to EU citizens only?

Remembering the past is important when we talk about the future of Europe.

In Ireland, many people know about migration from their own history. A great deal of 'the Irish experience' was related to emigration, with people searching for a better life elsewhere, escaping poverty and conflicts, making a living, finding a job. The migration experience is not an easy one: the risk of exploitation, the task of adapting to a new culture and way of life, present challenges that mean migration is not as simple as people who have never moved sometimes may think. The current experience of Ireland – and it is a very recent one – is that of immigration: in a short period of time Ireland has become host to so many nationalities. Becoming a host and living with diverse cultures is different from the experience of being 'the other' elsewhere. An amount of learning and adaptation is today required of what was formerly a fairly homogenous society – a change which many people would not have thought possible just a few years back. This does create problems in society. At the same time, many Irish people have relatives in other countries and continents, and thus perhaps an easier access to understanding what it means to live as a minority, and what integration and diversity entail.

Development of Migration Policies in the EU

An underlying principle and value of the European Union is the freedom of movement for the citizens of the Union. All EU citizens, and members of their families, have the right to travel to, reside in, and take up employment or self-employed activity in any of the EU Member States – with some exceptions, or rather restrictions, still in place for the citizens of eight of the ten new Member States who joined in May 2004.[2] Freedom of movement is aimed at increasing the mobility and flexibility of EU citizens within the EU and at opening borders not only for goods but for people.

In the 1980s, when decisions regarding the freedom of movement of EU citizens were taken, fears were expressed that opening the borders could lead to uncontrollable immigration. There was particular concern that people from countries outside the EU could use their entry into one Member Country to move on to another Member Country. Thus, common rules for issuing entry visas were agreed. Even today, Ireland and the UK are not party to the Schengen Agreement which established a free travel area, without border controls.

Since the 1980s, a common European migration and asylum policy has been envisaged. However, in the countries of the former fifteen-member EU the national rules for entry and residence of migrants from third countries, as well as the systems for dealing with the applications of asylum seekers, still remain rather diverse, so persons who receive a visa or residence permit from one country may not receive it from another, and vice versa. To make matters worse, asylum seekers are sometimes not granted the refugee status that they would be accorded in another Member State with a more thorough asylum procedure in place.

An Area of Freedom, Security and Justice

With the EU Treaty of Amsterdam, which entered into force in 1999, the EU gained competence in the fields of migration and asylum. Until that time, common rules and procedures were exclusively agreed between the respective ministries of the Member States, sometimes, but not at all systematically, involving national parliaments. Since 1999, the European Parliament has had to be consulted and the European Commission has the right to make proposals for EU legislation, as well as power to control the implementation of legislation. Until 2004, the Ministers of Justice and Home Affairs had to agree unanimously on all legislation. Now, however, we have entered a new era: legislation can be adopted by qualified majority voting (except in the case of labour immigration) and the European Parliament has to agree under the co-decision procedure.

The first time the Heads of Government of EU Member States dealt with EU migration and asylum policy was in 1999. The Summit of Tampere (Finland) is rightly regarded as a turning point towards a more realistic migration policy. For the first time, it was acknowledged that EU Member States would need immigration in the future and thus the Heads of Government agreed that common rules for entry and residence of migrants ought to be elaborated (Council of the European Union, 1999, n. 10–27). An approximation of the rights of third-country nationals to the rights of EU citizens was regarded as fundamental to facilitating social integration (n. 21). However, common measures against irregular migration and for expulsion were also envisaged. In relation to asylum, a common European policy, based on the Geneva Convention on Refugees and its related protocol, was envisaged: common rules for temporary protection, a common definition of persons recognised as refugees or otherwise in need of international protection, common rules for asylum procedures and reception conditions of asylum seekers.

The European Commission took up the challenge of the Tampare Summit and in November 1999 presented draft measures against discrimination. In December 1999, the Commission presented a Council Directive to realise the right to family reunification of third-country nationals.[3] A proposal for temporary protection in the case of a major influx of refugees – against the background of the crises in Bosnia and Kosovo – was fairly speedily agreed by the Council of Ministers. The proposals of the years 1999–2001 were written in the spirit of Tampere and aimed at a harmonisation of standards and rights. However, this objective has not been met in the process of negotiations since that time.

Migration Policy as a Security Policy?

Since the criminal attacks of 11 September 2001 in the US,[4] common security policy and 'anti-terrorism' policy have gained priority over migration and asylum policy. These policies are driven by the concepts of control and restriction. In particular, the issuing of visas and the storage and exchange of data between authorities are vigorously pursued in the Council of Ministers, and it seems that infringements of the rights of persons are regarded as a necessity. Persons of foreign origin, particularly those from countries where the majority population is Muslim, are now under general suspicion. The principle of law that there should exist a reasonable suspicion before an individual's freedom can be restricted is increasingly undermined. For asylum seekers, specific security measures, such as electronic 'tags', are being considered. This is despite the fact that already people who are making an application for asylum have to present their personal data, curricula vitae and their history of persecution. Moreover, under EURODAC regulations, they have their fingerprints taken (Council of the European Union, 2000).

As a consequence of these developments, a huge amount of data is stored and exchanged; entry and departure of third-country nationals is registered and saved; the issue or denial of a visa is stored in a special database. Experiments are underway with new technologies for the registration of additional biometric personal data. In addition, the deportation of potentially criminal third-country nationals is being debated. In the UK, consideration is even being given to suspending the validity of protection clauses and rights enshrined in the European Convention on Human Rights for persons from third countries. Whether these measures can increase security is more than questionable. But such measures certainly contribute to the feeling of insecurity in societies. The EU Monitoring Centre on Racism and Xenophobia has reported that violence against Muslim and Jewish institutions has increased. Populist right-wing parties are using fear to stir further anxieties against foreigners. As control measures by states are also based on a general suspicion of third-country nationals, they prepare the ground on which racism is flourishing and the potential for conflict and violence increasing.

EU Immigration Policy

Parallel to the development of control mechanisms, some consideration of immigration is continuing in the EU. This is against the background of the demographic situation in the majority of the twenty-five EU Member States, which will experience a population decline and an increase in the percentage of older people in the coming years. As the originally proposed rules for entry and residence in the EU were not adopted, the European Commission presented, in January 2005, a Green Paper on economic migration 'to launch a process of in-depth discussion, involving the EU institutions, Members States and the civil society, on the most appropriate form of Community rules for admitting economic migrants and on the added value of adopting such a common framework' (European Commission, 2005, p. 3).

In most EU countries, there are economic sectors in need of qualified personnel, particularly the health and care services, crafts, hotels and restaurants, as well as agriculture. In these sectors there are already significant numbers of workers from third countries. This is true not only of the 'old' EU Member States, but also of 'new' Member States. While the internationalisation of labour markets increases, legislation is lagging behind. Legal entry and employment is often so complicated – and decisions sometimes so arbitrary – that many third-country nationals turn to people smugglers, paying them for the trip and for papers, as well as for finding a job, rather than using legal channels. This entails great risk for those who often find themselves in a precarious situation of dependence.

It is vital to increase the rights-based security of third-country nationals in order to establish trust in authorities and the decisions they make. An important step on the way is the regularisation of persons in irregular situations, as has been undertaken several times in Italy, France, Belgium, Greece and Spain. The recent regularisation in Spain aimed at creating regular jobs is directed at the 'shadow economy'. It will be important to have a close look at this new approach and evaluate it carefully. We may find that measures to improve the position of third-country nationals are far more effective than enormous control mechanisms at the borders. Regular jobs entail security for employees as well as participation in social security and tax systems. There are potential benefits for the whole of society from this type of approach, which are too often neglected in the design of migration policies.

Common rules, new and stable monitoring and coordination mechanisms for immigration into the EU could be important steps on the way towards transparent and open migration legislation, which would help to reduce irregular migration (and employment within the shadow economy).

Refugee Protection in the EU

The Member States of the EU have stated their commitment to protect refugees in the EU in accordance with the Geneva Convention on Refugees and related treaties. This commitment was included in the EU draft Constitutional Treaty, in Article III–267.[5] In November 2004, the Council of Ministers adopted an amended Directive for common standards for asylum procedures. At the end of September 2005, the European Parliament adopted a report that was critical of many of the provisions of the Directive (European Parliament, Committee on Civil Liberties, Justice and Home Affairs, 2005).

Nevertheless, the Council disregarded the opinion of the European Parliament and issued the Directive on 1 December 2005 without any amendments having been made (Council of the European Union, 2005). In early 2006, the European Parliament decided to refer the Directive to the European Court of Justice for a ruling.

This Directive could effectively exclude many asylum seekers from a determination procedure. The travel route of the asylum seeker would determine whether the person would be eligible to enter the asylum procedure at all. Already at land borders, at airports and at seaports, an accelerated – and thus not complete – procedure is being implemented under which a decision can be taken as to whether a person is to be allowed access to a full asylum determination procedure and thus to protection. It is argued that this 'compromise' would open the way for future asylum regulations under qualified majority voting as well as co-decision procedures with the European Parliament. But the United Nations High Commissioner for Refugees (2005) as well as NGOs and Churches regard this Directive as extremely problematic as it could effectively exclude refugees from the protection to which they should be entitled.

In November 2004, the European Council adopted 'The Hague Programme' to further develop the area of freedom, justice and security (Council of the European Union, 2004). Under the Programme, while the Common European Asylum System is to be further developed (n. 1.3), the Council also proposes to work for the resettlement of asylum seekers from other regions to Europe, and to consider asylum determination outside the territory of the EU. The British Prime Minister, Tony Blair, had already suggested asylum determination procedures outside EU territory. That proposal had, however, been withdrawn after a feasibility study had pointed to many problems. In 2004, the then German Federal Interior Minister, Otto Schilly, re-opened the debate, and the issue is being pursued without very concrete proposals. This debate is often confused with the establishment in Libya of Italian camps for deportees, which were bilaterally agreed in 2004. Under this agreement, Italy is deporting hundreds of asylum seekers to Libya – where they supposedly come from – and paying for their accommodation in camps in Libya. In turn, Italy pressed successfully in the EU for the lifting of economic sanctions against Libya. As Libya is not party to the Geneva Convention on Refugees, these deportations, without any chance for an asylum determination procedure, are regarded by many organisations in Italy and other European countries as being in contravention of the law. This is an issue that should be looked into by the Council of Europe in Strasbourg.

What is the Value of an EU Migration and Asylum Policy?

Currently, EU migration and asylum policies are contradictory and ambiguous. We see more restrictions, an increase in expulsions and deportations, the detention of people who have not committed a crime and far too many dying at Europe's borders. Migration and asylum policies are characterised by national self-interest and localised views; truly common policies, transparency, the rule of law extended in the interest of third-country nationals, are only slowly developing.

Management of migration, including regulations concerning visas and work permits, is still understood as control. This approach is maintained despite the fact that migration between Member States (with the exception of eight of the new Member States) inside the EU has been regulated in a far better way than any system of border control. One could say that internal EU migration offers a success story for managing migration, based on the freedom of movement of people and their right to family life. With internal migration there are, of course, some problems – for example, regarding integration, access to the labour market, recognition of qualifications. But these problems are tackled not with laws to introduce new restrictions, but with social and integration programmes. This is also the response needed for third-country nationals. The issue of integration would then no longer be tackled by granting or withdrawing a residence status, but by providing services appropriate to meeting needs. Migration and integration policies require management of diversity and also services which assist societies to change and adapt, rather than putting the burden of success or failure of integration solely on the shoulders of third-country nationals.

If the good practice that is a feature of the EU's internal migration management could be introduced into a common policy towards third countries and third-country nationals, and if a policy could be developed which respected the rights of the person, honoured the contribution of migrants to our societies and invested in relations with third countries, rather than pressing them towards controlling emigration, then the EU would gain in terms of security, respect and solidarity. Furthermore, it would then be possible for the EU to uphold these values – which are fundamental to the Union – with greater credibility in international fora. An important building block would be the ratification of the International Convention on the Rights of all Migrant Workers and Members of their Families, which entered into force in 2003.

International migration and living together in diversity are challenges for our future that cannot be addressed with national policies alone. The EU has far more to offer than creating a fortress. However, it seems that, at present, the fears and worries of people and politicians lead us further away from a common vision for the EU and the people living on its territory. Particularly in the current political debate, it requires tremendous courage, especially of politicians, to pursue consistently a European policy that respects human rights and upholds solidarity, justice and freedom of movement as fundamental values.

Notes

1. This paper was presented at the conference, *The Future of Europe: Uniting Vision, Values and Citizens?*, held in Dublin on 27 September 2005.
2. These eight countries are: Czech Republic, Estonia, Hungary, Latvia, Lithuania, Poland, Slovakia, Slovenia. There are no restrictions for Cyprus and Malta.
3. The final draft of the Directive on Family Reunification was approved by the Council of Ministers on 22 September 2003 (Council of the European Union, 2003). Member states were required to transpose the Directive into national legislation by 3 October 2005.
4. The definition of the attacks as a crime is preferred to the label 'terrorist'. Current law provides for sufficient means to sentence criminals and, in

the case of the attacks on the World Trade Centre, for a sentence for mass murder, if persons are found guilty. However, the concept of 'war on terror' is outside the judicial system and poses a severe threat to international human rights standards.

5. Article III–267 of the draft Constitution states: 'The Union shall develop a common policy on asylum, subsidiary protection and temporary protection with a view to offering appropriate status to any third-country national requiring international protection and ensuring compliance with the principle of non-refoulement. This policy must be in accordance with the Geneva Convention of 28 July 1951 and the Protocol of 31 January 1967 relating to the status of refugees, and other relevant treaties.' (Part III, Chapter IV, Section 2, 'Policies on Border Checks, Asylum and Immigration')

References

Council of the European Union (1999) *Presidency Conclusions: Tempere European Council,* 15 and 16 October 1999.

Council of the European Union (2000) 'Council Regulation (EC) No 2725/2000 of 11 December 2000 'Concerning the Establishment of 'Eurodac' for Comparison of Fingerprints for the Effective Application of the Dublin Convention', *Official Journal of the European Union,* L 316, 15.12.2005, pp. 1–10.

Council of the European Union (2003) 'On the Right to Family Reunification', *Official Journal of the European Union,* L 251, 3.10.2003, pp. 12–18.

Council of the European Union (2005) 'The Hague Programme: Strengthening Freedom, Security and Justice in the European Union' in *Presidency Conclusions, Brussels European Council, 4/5 November 2004,* Brussels, 8.12.2004, 14292/1/04, Annex 1.

Council of the European Union (2005) 'Council Directive 2005/85/EC of 1 December 2005 on Minimum Procedures in Member States for Granting and Withdrawing Refugee Status', *Official Journal of the European Union,* L 326, 13.12.2005, pp. 13–34.

Commission of the European Communities (2005) *Green Paper on an EU Approach to Managing Economic Migration,* Brussels, 11.1.2005, COM (2004) 811 final.

European Parliament, Committee on Civil Liberties (2005) Justice and Home Affairs, *Report on the Amended Proposal for a Council Directive on Minimum Standards on Procedures in Member States for Granting and Withdrawing*

Refugee Status (14203/2004 – C6-0200/2004 – 2000/0238 (CNS)), 29.9.2005, Rapporteur: Wolfgang Kreissl-Döörfler, Session document, FINAL, A6-0222.

United Nations High Commissioner for Refugees (2005) *UNHCR Provisional Comments on the Proposal for a Council Directive on Minimum Standards on Procedures in Member States for Granting and Withdrawing Refugee Status*, 10 February 2005. (www.unhcr.org)

The Future of Europe

A Shared Responsibility for Church and Politics

Noel Treanor

Europeans are currently wrestling with numerous aspects of their continent's future identity. The debate on the European Union Constitutional Treaty, ratified by fourteen of the twenty-five Member States and thus by a majority of EU citizens, though rejected by France and The Netherlands in referenda, is but one in an ensemble of issues which are determinative for the future. To the crucial matter of how, and to what extent, our nations share sovereignty in order to pursue the values and objectives of the European project, in a world context that is ever more determined by globalisation and unlimited forms of interdependence, must be added several other issues decisive for Europe's future identity.

Among these key concerns is the challenge of boosting economic growth and competitiveness in tandem with social cohesion and environmental protection (the Lisbon Strategy). Likewise, there is the emergent question of the borders of Europe, the limits to enlargement and the search for new forms of relationships with neighbouring countries. The challenge of developing a policy on migration and related issues which fosters and protects human rights, whilst consolidating security and promoting integration in our multi-cultural societies, has acquired a new and acute urgency for both the Member States and the EU. In order to adequately address challenges facing our societies, whether in the economic, social, scientific and social ethical fields, Europeans and their political leaders urgently need to endow the EU with the political means to exercise its weight on the world stage.

These and other issues began to crystallise as the EU experienced its historic enlargement towards central and eastern Europe on 1 May 2004. Whether or not perceived as enlargement, they required and still require attention and resolution. As it happens, that resolution can be advanced by the current historic moment, for on 25 March 2007 the twenty-five Member States of the EU will mark fifty years since the Treaty of Rome which established the European Economic Community (EEC). The historic and qualitative political option achieved and sealed in that treaty between the six founder European nations (together with the treaty establishing the European Atomic Energy Community (EURATOM), signed on the same date, and the earlier Treaty of Paris, establishing the European Coal and Steel Community, which was signed on 18 April 1951) opened the way, and above all provided for the institutions, which would set Europe, its nations and peoples on a new political trajectory. It would consolidate peace within and between the Member States. It would prove that it was possible for the Member States to pool sovereignty in ever-widening circles of policy fields. It would also show that whilst applying the principle of subsidiarity, they could achieve a *community method* for policy-making which would boost the quality of life of the Member States, the regions and their citizens and offer a determinative perspective to neighbouring countries. It would also enact solidarity not just as a regulating principle for the organisation of the market, the economy and the social sector, but also as its key political method. Thus, the balance of power politics of an earlier period was replaced by a politics of solidarity between the nations, and between the great and the small nations. This remains a key and identifying aim of the EU, of its institutional arrangements and checks and balances, and indeed of the Constitutional Treaty.

Understanding and Owning Europe

Fifty years on, the success of the European project deserves celebration. But over and above celebration it is in need of civic recognition and understanding. It needs a narrative. The almost constitutive paradox at the heart of the EU is that despite the success of the post-war European project, as citizens we have not succeeded in *understanding and owning* Europe and its political institutions as *our* instruments for making the world a better place in which to live. The fact is that Europe with its institutional arrangements has made a qualitative difference to our lives, to European history and to the emerging world order. Fifty years on, citizens of the Member States need to seize this fact. Indeed, they must be helped to appreciate the achievement and significance of this still fragile European project. A diversified programme of civic education on Europe, promoted cooperatively by public, private and voluntary sectors, is urgently needed throughout all the Member States. New, creative and effective initiatives are urgently needed to bring the European ideal to the citizens. Such is the precondition for a broad and informed civic ownership of the European project, an essential ingredient to its continuing success in the new information society.

On the part of the Christian Churches, there are countless initiatives throughout the Member States to explore the significance of the European ideal and to investigate, from the angle of Christian anthropology, the social–ethical quality of the EU's policy responses to the challenges it faces within and beyond its borders.[1] These initiatives can make a vital contribution to a narrative, at once civic and Christian, regarding European construction. Such a narrative is essential to building a sense of responsibility for Europe and its future among Christians who are citizens of Member States characterised by both their common heritage and their historical, cultural, and political diversities.

These initiatives also constitute a contribution to the debate on the future of Europe, called for at the June 2005 meeting of the European Council in the aftermath of the results in the French and Dutch referenda. Since the Single European Act (1986) in particular, much effort has been expended to promote and spread such a debate. As of autumn 2005, the European Commission has published two papers in the hope of kick-starting a public debate throughout the twenty-five Member States (Commission of the European Communities, 2005; 2006). In this respect, throughout Europe the Churches will continue to offer space to believers and also to non-believers to explore the vitally important question of Europe's future. At the European level, the Christian Churches launched in January 2006 a process leading to the Third European Ecumenical Encounter, which will reach its conclusion in a meeting of delegates of the Churches in Sibiu, Romania, in September 2007. Among its nine fora at least three will address issues directly concerned with the shape of the future EU and the contents of its policies.

Some Core Elements of the Catholic Church's View of Europe

In order to set out some of the seminal aspects of how the Catholic Church considers the European Union, a review of the Apostolic Exhortation of Pope John Paul II (2003), *Ecclesia in Europa*, may be helpful. Rooted in the deliberations of the Second Special Assembly of the Synod of Bishops for Europe,[2] the document brings together some of the key emphases which have emerged in papal and ecclesial thinking on Europe in recent decades.

In *Ecclesia in Europa* – consonant with papal thinking from Pius XII onwards, and in particular with the deliberations of the First Special Assembly of the Synod of Bishops for Europe held in 1999 just after the fall of the Berlin Wall[3] – Europe is conceived of in terms wider than the European Union. Thus Europe is described as a '… *primarily cultural and historical concept*, which denotes a reality born as a continent thanks also to the unifying force of Christianity, which has been capable of integrating peoples and cultures among themselves and which is intimately linked to the whole of European culture.' (n. 108) The Exhortation's diagnosis of Europe's spiritual condition reveals a tension, as it points to an ambiguity in the European consciousness. Contemporary Europe, *Ecclesia in Europa* suggests, needs also 'to make a qualitative leap in becoming conscious of its spiritual heritage' (n. 120) because of the loss of Europe's Christian memory and heritage (n. 7) and because the predominant culture gives the impression of a 'silent apostasy' (n. 9).

On the matter of the relationship between Church and state, between the Christian faith and public authority, the document explicitly states that the Church 'is not calling for a return to the confessional state' (n. 117). It asserts that the Church fully respects the secular nature of the European institutions (n. 114). While thus recognising the separation between the religious and the political realms, the document affirms the importance of a 'healthy co-operation between the ecclesial community and political society' (n. 117). It goes on to underline that the Church *can make a unique contribution* to the prospect of unification by offering the European institutions, in continuity with her tradition and in fidelity to the principles of her social teaching, the engagement of believing communities committed to bringing about the humanization of society on the basis of the Gospel, lived under the sign of hope.' (n. 117)

Europe's spiritual vocation to promote universal values, solidarity and peace in the world is underlined in the final chapter of *Ecclesia in Europa*. In this, the document echoes the sentiments of the Schuman Declaration of 9 May 1950 and indeed the vision of the founding fathers of the European project as sketched in the preambles to the founding treaties, referred to earlier. In a similar vein, *Ecclesia in Europa* propounds: 'Saying "Europe" must be equivalent to saying "openness" ... it needs to be an *open and welcoming Continent*, continuing to develop in the current process of globalization forms of cooperation which are not merely economic but social and cultural as well.' (n. 111) Thus, 'Europe cannot close in on itself' and it 'cannot and must not lose interest in the rest of the world' (n. 111) and it must 'become an active partner in promoting and implementing a globalization in solidarity' which, the document asserts, requires a globalisation of solidarity (n. 112). And in this respect the Exhortation emphasises that Christian inspiration 'is capable of transforming political, cultural and economic groupings into a form of coexistence in which all Europeans will feel at home and will form a family of nations from which other areas of the world can draw fruitful inspiration.' (n. 121) This latter affirmation is also noteworthy in that it rightly adverts to the fact that the process of European integration and unification evokes admiration on the part of nations in other regions of the world. (For example, it inspired the evolution of the African Union.) However, Europe's capacity to endure and to act as a credible model will depend on decisions on the meta issues of the value systems and social–ethical principles which determine its policy choices.

Precisely in order to offer contributions informed by this Christian inspiration to shape Europe, 'the presence of Christians, properly trained and competent, is needed in the various European agencies and institutions, in order to contribute – with respect for the correct dynamics of democracy and through an exchange of proposals – to the shaping of a European social order which is increasingly respectful of every man and woman, and thus in accordance with the common good.' (n. 117) Democracy and dialogue are accepted by the Church as core elements of the European political process. It is also recognised that all contributions to debate in the political arena are made 'in the context of the ethical and religious pluralism which increasingly characterizes Europe' (n. 20). A pre-eminent and guiding aim for Christian contributions to debate on the multiple policy fields is to ensure that Europe is not 'exclusively subject to the law of the marketplace, but resolutely determined to safeguard the dignity of the human person also in social and economic relations.' (n. 87)

The central and constitutive significance of the Christian heritage to Europe's identity is a leitmotiv of the text: 'Christian faith belongs, in a radical and decisive way, to the foundations of European culture.' (n. 108) Hence the request of Pope John Paul II that 'a reference to the religious and in particular Christian heritage of Europe' (n. 114) be included in the Treaty Establishing a Constitution for Europe. As we now know, the word religious was included in the Preamble, a remarkable advance on the Preamble to the Charter of Fundamental Rights drafted some four years earlier, adopted at the Council of Nice and now integrated in the Constitutional Treaty in its second part. Pope John Paul II further requested that three 'complementary elements' should be recognised in the Treaty:

the right of Churches and religious communities to organize themselves freely in conformity with their statutes and proper convictions; respect for the specific identity of the different religious confessions and provision for a structured dialogue between the European Union and those confessions; and respect for the juridical status already enjoyed by Churches and religious institutions by virtue of the legislation of the member states of the Union. (n. 114)

It may be worth observing that the term 'religious communities' here refers to religions and/or faith communities which accept such basic givens of organised society as democracy, the rule of law and human rights, and are recognised by the Member States. In this passage of *Ecclesia in Europa*, Pope John Paul II spearheaded and reiterated proposals supported and advanced ecumenically by all Christian Churches to the Convention on the Future of Europe for inclusion in the text of the Treaty. All of these elements are to be found in Article I–52 of the Constitutional Treaty. In terms of constitutional and civil ecclesiastical law this was a major development. Indeed the inclusion of its provisions has been referred to as something of a revolution (von Vietinghoff, 2004). It is, however, also the result of numerous developments, particularly the practice of informal dialogue which evolved in the 1990s between the Churches and the European Commission (and also with the European Parliament) and the emerging culture of intensified consultation on the part of the EU institutions in pursuit of good governance.

Furthermore, Article I–52 had become a necessity for EU primary law itself because of the corpus of secondary EU law regarding religion which had been developed by the EU and its institutions over the decades.[4] Necessary it may have been, but it was a necessity which engendered intense debate in the Convention on the Future of Europe and in the public arena on the meaning of *laïcité* for contemporary European society. For the Catholic Church, the Orthodox Churches, and the Churches of the Reformation, the regular, open and transparent dialogue between the Churches and the EU foreseen by Article I–52 is an instrument which ensures the right of the religious voice to be heard in the consort of European public policy debate. It is a gateway to fulfilling their responsibility *vis à vis* Europe's political institutions; it is not a privilege.

A novum in *Ecclesia in Europa*, and barely noticeable in the English language version, more of a hint than an assertion, but nonetheless pregnant with meaning, is worth noting: the document attributes to the *Church in Europe* the quality of a subject with responsibility for preaching the Word of God, celebrating the liturgy and for concrete political diaconia (n. 26, 45, 65, 66, 69, 105, 124). Bishops to whom the text is primarily addressed, and indeed all Christians, are challenged to think and assume responsibility for Europe. How can Christians give life and content to this concept of *Church in Europe* as an acting subject? Something of a new horizon, though historians may be inclined to smile gently, it will nevertheless require inventiveness and imagination so that our local Churches may reach beyond long-established comfort lines in thought and practice limiting us to national boundaries.

Some further elements of an ecclesiology for Europe set out in the text may be noted. Suffice is to recall the emphasis on the ecumenical imperative reinforced by the process of European integration and unification (n. 17, 30, 31, 32, 54) and the four challenges for evangelisation set out in chapter five: the family (n. 90), human life (n. 96), building a society worthy of the human person (n. 97–8), immigration and a culture of acceptance (n. 100–3).

These are some of the central elements of the Church's commitment to the European project as set out in *Ecclesia in Europa*. That document is, as already noted, the result of the Synodal process to which the members of the Synod, chiefly bishops from all countries in Europe, contributed. It is worth remarking that the process also included input from invited religious and laity from numerous walks of life. As indicated above, as far as the European Union and its institutions are concerned, it presupposes interaction with them on the part of the Church. How then does the Church concretely interact with the European Union and its institutions?

Church Presence to the Institutions of the European Union

Whilst the post-war European project enjoyed the support of political leaders from all shades of the political spectrum, any objective reading of its origins must recognise the determinative contribution of Christian Democracy and the principles of Catholic social thought to the political theory and practice underpinning the process. In the course of five and more decades, Christians of all denominations, politicians, civil servants and other interested parties, have sought to promote and develop the European ideal out of a conviction fertilised by Christian social thinking. The project of the common market and the broader integration process were discerned as vectors for the realisation of fundamental human values in concrete economic and social terms.

As in the first decades of European construction, today Christian believers among the European officials and Members of the European Parliament try to enhance the human quality of European policy. Lest any misunderstanding arise in this regard, it should be stressed here that in this they do not act as clandestine agents of a Church, seeking to proselytise or confessionalise the political order. Their professional aim is to assist in elaborating quality policy which will promote the common good of all. Of course, this is not ignore the plurality of currents and forces wrestling to shape the European political order. Christians in public life are called through their daily professional competence and skills, enriched by Christian thought, their faith-inspired values, and their efforts, to shape the nuts and bolts of policy, to mould a just social order which fosters the common good. They do so in full respect for democratic institutions and their decision-making procedures.

This primary involvement in the European political process has been supported since the mid-twentieth century by Church-based organisations specialising, to a greater or lesser extent, in European affairs. The first to take shape was the Jesuit Catholic European

Study and Information Centre (OCIPE) set up in 1956 at the request of the then Bishop of Strasbourg to liaise with the Council of Europe.

The Holy See established diplomatic relations with the European Communities in 1970. As of that year, the Apostolic Nuncio to Belgium and Luxembourg exercised a second and separate role as Nuncio to the European Communities. This remained the case until 1996, when a Nunciature to the European Communities was established and an Apostolic Nuncio appointed. The Nunciature is a diplomatic representation and as such is the only Church body to have a status officially recognised by the European Communities.

The Commission of the Bishops' Conferences of the European Community (COMECE) was set up in 1980 and followed on from an information office established in 1976 (Service d'Information Pastorale Européenne Catholique, SIPECA). Today, its members are the twenty-two delegates, each a bishop, of the twenty-two episcopates on the territory of the twenty-five Member States. The Bishops' Conference of Switzerland has had observer status since the foundation of COMECE and the episcopates of candidate countries also have observer status. COMECE holds two plenary meetings per year to consider issues in EU policy. It is served by a secretariat, based in Brussels. Its core tasks are threefold: firstly, to monitor and make input to EU policy-making; secondly, through a monthly review, *Europe-Infos* (published in English, French, German and Polish) to make a modest contribution to building a European public opinion; thirdly, through conferences and seminars to promote debate on fundamental and long-term issues in European policy between Christian faith and politics. Through its secretariat, which maintains contact with the secretariats of the episcopal conferences in the Member States, and with the support of specialists in numerous policy fields and scientific disciplines, COMECE seeks to provide a discerning, and when necessary critical, support for the European project.

Another element of the Church's presence to the European institutions takes the form of nascent think-tanks on European issues. The Jesuit initiative, OCIPE, having originated in Strasbourg, in 1968 established an antenna in Brussels to focus on EC issues. After the fall of the Berlin Wall, further antennae were set up in Budapest and Warsaw. In 1995, the Dominican Order launched a comparable initiative, Spirituality, Cultures and Society in Europe (ESPACES), with centres in Brussels, Berlin and Warsaw. Both initiatives operate as networks. Their main objective is to contribute to debates on key issues in European policy through conferences, participation in public discussion and publications. To a large extent, they seek to apply their traditional charisms to the European process through a range of mainly academic initiatives aimed at disseminating ideas, provoking public debate and helping to build up an informed European public opinion.

Other Catholic organisations work on single policy fields. Chief among these are Caritas Europa which focuses on social policy, the Africa Europe Faith and Justice Network (AEFJN) dealing with EU policy regarding Africa, the Jesuit Refugee Service (JRS) which has an active office in Brussels working on migration and refugee policy, and the Centre for International Development Cooperation and Solidarity (CIDSE) which includes EU development policy in its field of work.

More recently, the religious congregations have set up a small office (UCESM) in Brussels which aims to assist congregations throughout Europe to achieve a European dimension in their activities both within the EU and in the pan-European context of their missions.

Notable also is the presence of Catholic media to the EU institutions, whether in the form of the German, *Katholische Nachrichten Agentur* (KNA), the Italian, *SIR-Europa*, or individual correspondents working for Catholic newspapers. They strive to thematise and report on EU issues. Indeed the Catholic press throughout Europe could probably make greater use of their pioneering work and thus contribute to developing an informed Catholic public opinion on EU policy issues, both in the draft stage and after adoption.

The Conferences of European Churches (CEC), at present made up of 125 Churches, brings together the Anglican Church, the Reformed Churches and the Orthodox Churches in Europe. Its Commission for Church and Society engages in much the same kind of work as COMECE. Other autonomous Churches-linked organisations specialise in migration policy (the Churches' Commission for Migrants in Europe, CCME), development policy (Association of World Council of Churches related Development Organisations in Europe, APRODEV), and social policy (EURODIACONIA).

For their part, the Orthodox Churches have established independent offices to liaise with the EU: the Ecumenical Patriarchate in 1995, the Orthodox Church of Greece in 2000, and the Patriarchate of Moscow in 2001.

COMECE has played a key role in building an interface between Church and the EU institutions. In doing so, it cooperated ecumenically, and continues to do so, with the relevant organisations of the other Christian Churches. This interface with the EU, still in the early phase of its life, was not a given, or self-evident from the beginning of the Church presence to the European institutions. It had to be grown from tender seedlings. The Churches were not invited by the European institutions to monitor or make input to their work. Rather, enlightened Church leaders, sometimes at the suggestion of men and women working in the institutions, understood the unique significance of the European project and saw in it a new quality of politics deserving discernment and critical support from the Christian community. They proactively decided to establish a presence to the institutions of the European Communities (EC) to establish contacts and to engage in informal exchange and discussions mostly with individual civil servants, politicians and members of the European Commission.

Until after the Single European Act, and effectively until after 1989, the initiative to make contact with the European institutions lay with the Churches. Dialogue with the Churches was not sought after by the EC. The milieu of its institutions was determined primarily by the French administrative system. In so far as the relationship with Churches and religions was concerned, the French model of *laïcité* was thought to be unquestionable and the only model viable for Europe's future. However, forces from within the EC itself, the significant advance represented by the Single European Act, and the impulses to further political integration guided by Jacques Delors as President of the European Commission, combined with forces towards European re-unification set loose by the events of winter 1989 to require a re-appraisal of the vision of the founding fathers. Delors and other leaders realised the urgent need to shape a public narrative on the meaning of the European project. Thus, in the early 1990s as part of an effort to engage *les instances de sens* in discussing the shape and nature of Europe, President Delors initiated twice-yearly dialogue seminars with the Churches on European issues. This was a presidential initiative without a formal legal basis. The practice was continued under his successors, Presidents Jacques Santer and Romano Prodi. Its significance lay in the fact that it was the first step on the part of an EU institution to enter into dialogue with the Churches, as communities of faith and as significant actors in their own right in society. A process of interaction had begun. The proactive work of the Churches in the previous years had irrigated the ground for encounter.

Further developments were to follow, most notably Declaration no. 11 on the status of Churches which was annexed to the Treaty of Amsterdam.[5] Thereafter, in a series of steps, including the *White Paper on European Governance* (Commission of the European Communities, 2001), and in Communications of the European Commission on a strengthened culture of consultation, the Churches were taken into account as participants in dialogue. Like the earlier steps, these were staging posts on the way to Article I–52 of the Constitutional Treaty which foresees a constitutionally recognised dialogue with the Churches, the communities of faith and the humanist tradition.[6]

Even though the secondary law of the European Communities developed what is effectively an embryonic corpus of European legal dispositions on religion, the EC institutions, as already noted, were slow and tentative in taking any steps to provide a juridical basis for an interface with Churches and religions. Whilst formal implementation of Article I–52 must await the ratification of the Constitutional Treaty, new and complex challenges in areas such as culture, migration, integration policy, security issues and terrorism have led many responsible for EU policy-making to consult and exchange with Churches and faith communities.[7] Effective governance of contemporary pluri-cultural and pluri-religious society requires as much.

However, the achievement of such qualitative governance requires an informed citizenry which participates actively in public life. Indeed, the further success of the European project will depend in great part on the capacity of EU citizens to seize the need of each Member State for the European project and its institutions. Only thus will they engender and consolidate the political will necessary to give renewed impetus to the project as the means by which the nations and peoples of Europe together address the global challenges confronting all our societies. In other words, fostering the European project requires tackling the much-lamented democratic deficit and developing an appreciation of the integral European dimension of our sense of citizenship.

Fostering a Sense of European Citizenship

To date, European citizenship, in so far as it is apprehended, is experienced and understood in terms of a series of rights for citizens of the EU: freedom of movement and residence within the EU, the right to vote and to stand as a candidate in elections to the European Parliament, the right to vote and to stand as a candidate at municipal elections in the Member State in which one resides, diplomatic and consular protection from any Member State in a third country where one's country is not represented. European citizenship has also acquired a new quality from the Charter of

Fundamental Rights of the EU, integrated into the Constitutional Treaty. Notwithstanding these rights, immense civic and cultural educational efforts are needed to generate a sense of European citizenship commensurate with the significance and success of the European project.

To this end, and to provide Catholics with a tool to trigger reflection and debate on the subject, COMECE has published a text entitled, *The Evolution of the European Union and the Responsibility of Catholics.*[8] In the first chapter, the document reflects on the significance of the European project, and in particular it re-reads the Schuman Declaration of 9 May 1950 from the vantage point of the 2004 historic enlargement to central and eastern Europe. Thus, it asserts that:

> ... in re-reading what enabled the birth of the Union, as well as its present development, we shall discover that the Union, before being a large market and an institutional construction, was at first the result of a political act in the noblest sense of the term. (n. 8)

The document points out that the prophetic quality of the founding vision with peace as its aim, freedom of access as a basic principle, and solidarity as its method is still little known, unfortunately. It merits re-appraisal today since many Europeans, including Catholics, do not see how solidarity can transcend the nation (n. 23).

The second chapter considers the experience of central and eastern Europe and especially the events of 1989 which ended the communist system. In a few pages, it evokes a different and painful period of our common European history, all too little known in the west. 'We are dying for Hungary and for Europe': thus commented the telex transmitted worldwide by the Director of the Hungarian press agency as Russian tanks entered Budapest in November 1956 (n. 31). The experience of the other part of Europe also confirms that: 'The teaching of history – and of all of history, with its many complexities – constitutes a definitive precursor to European citizenship.' (n. 26) A crucial contribution to the future of the EU will consist in peacefully working towards a common understanding of a history which is full of conflict yet common to us all (n. 32).

The final chapter explores how the spiritual, religious and sacramental experience of believers can motivate and sustain the civic engagement of European citizens. Challenging perspectives are evoked regarding the contribution Catholic communities might make to enhance the civic vitality of Europe. This leads on to a consideration of three core elements of Catholic social teaching from which the new Europe can draw inspiration: (i) maintaining unity in diversity, (ii) the separation between the religious and political spheres, whilst promoting a healthy relationship between them, (iii) the Christian faith's perspective regarding the eschatological Kingdom of God, which prevents illusions of a closure of history or the attainment of perfection by any political or economic order.

For Christians, as citizens, the challenges arising from European integration have a spiritual dimension: advancing towards the Kingdom of God is inseparable from service – of whatever form – to the political community (n. 44). The text acknowledges that the Christian faith is not to be identified with any political order (n. 42) and that the Church does not promote any particular political model (n. 36). At the same time, and in accordance with the Church's social teaching, it recognises that 'political engagement is important for our faith and our faith is important for our political engagement.' (n. 42) As members of the European body politic, Christians can provide a vital impulse to ensure that the European project responds to the ethical–political and spiritual vision of its founders. The text suggests that Christians have a particular responsibility in this respect, given the values at the root of the European project and the objectives to which it aspires. The common market, and forms of measured political integration, were not ends in themselves, or sophisticated forms of power games. They were, and remain, efforts to build a community of values, capable of exercising political power to promote peace and justice within Europe and beyond its borders. As human constructs, the EU's political arrangements and institutions will ever be in need of improvement and reform. Europe's future will depend in ever-greater measure on the political will of its citizens for the project to succeed, and on their comprehension of its necessity for the future viability of their regions and nations.

Taking Responsibility for our Future

When the preparation of the COMECE document began in autumn 2002, the Convention on the Future of Europe had accomplished eight months of work. By mid-June 2003, it would deliver the result of its work to the Italian Presidency. The draft for the Constitutional Treaty was amended by the Intergovernmental Conference under the EU Presidencies of Italy (July–December 2003) and Ireland (January–June 2004). The text of the Treaty was duly signed in Rome on 29 October 2004.

In some ways these were heady times, at least for the political elite and initiated. Whilst common sense forewarned of possible difficulties for ratification in referenda in Member States where euro-scepticism was known to constitute a critical mass of public opinion, rejection of the Treaty by referendum in two founding Member States, France and The Netherlands, was not expected. Even if the outcomes of both referenda were more the result of protest against internal governmental policy than of fundamental opposition to the Constitutional Treaty, the ratification debates crystallised the public sense of complex questions relating to Europe's future to which neither they, nor their political leaders, seemed to be capable of developing adequate responses. The enlargement of the Union to include Turkey, how to determine Europe's borders, the EU's capacity to integrate further members, Europe's economic competitiveness, its future social model, its demographic future, migration and integration policy, its future foreign policy: these constituted a whirlpool of issues requiring lucid political leadership and a European social consensus, indeed a social contract, as to the identity, objectives and limits of the new Europe. For many, the central question is: from where will this leadership come and how is such a European social consensus to be achieved?

An October–November 2005 Eurobarometer survey of public opinion in EU countries shows that despite weakening in the main indicators of support for the EU, the European public remains in favour of the Union's policies and supportive of the adoption of the Constitution (63 per cent). Support for EU membership stands at 50 per cent. Approximately a quarter of citizens feel involved in European affairs, while 47 per cent claim they would like to be more involved (Eurobarometer, 2005).

Europeans also expect the EU to advance policy in areas such as immigration, the fight against terrorism and in the foreign policy sphere (Eurobarometer, 2005a). In this respect, it is at least interesting to recall that on 27 May 2005, in the midst of the shock waves in the aftermath of the French 'No', seven EU Member States signed the Prüm Convention in order to deepen their cooperation in combating terrorism, organised crime and illegal immigration.[9] Like the earlier Schengen Agreement, this is an example of advanced cooperation between a group of Member States which surpasses existing EU treaty provisions. In taking this initiative in order to more effectively respond together to pressing societal problems, the signatory Member States pledged that the provisions of the treaty are to be applied in accordance with EU law. They also expressed the hope that other Member States will join them in due course and that the Prüm Convention may be incorporated into primary EU law in the future.

That this treaty passed almost unnoticed in summer 2005 is probably suggestive of how the European integration process will advance in the coming years – by short steps, oftentimes agreed and taken by groups of Member States which seek to advance together in fields where it is desirable and possible to act together. In the case of this treaty a not untypical problem arises, however. Here we see on the one side some governments and their civil services deciding to take such steps outside or alongside EU treaties and in intergovernmental mode, this being deemed the only possible means to advance in the face of a common problem. Inevitably, they provoke withering criticism from some political analysts who argue that such approaches produce negative externalities for the EU's area of freedom, security and justice, in that they circumvent the EU framework.

Whatever the merits and demerits of such initiatives, this approach will not resolve the problem of how to build up a European public opinion, girded by a sense of European identity and commitment to a political process based on an agreed set of values and objectives. The recent initiatives of the European Commission to communicate the European idea and to promote public debate admit as much. So far, these attempts would seem to have been stillborn. A more basic *prise de conscience* is needed if citizens are to be fired with enthusiasm for shaping a new Europe in line with the aspirations of the Schuman Declaration.

To facilitate such a development, it will be necessary to assist public opinion in apprehending that Europe has sources of a shared identity which pre-exist political constructs and are rooted to a great extent in its Christian heritage (Lustiger, 2006). It will be necessary also to show that the post-war European project is both a successful and noble political ideal susceptible to further social–ethical development for the good of Europe and the world, and that an informed and participative citizenry is a precondition of its further blossoming. Educational initiatives Europe-wide to address and elucidate the continuing need for the European project, enriched by the exchange of good practices, are therefore an urgently needed building stone for Europe's future. They will play an irreplaceable role in both creating an incubating space for European political leadership and for generating a European body politic at once aware of Europe's achievement and willing to shape it into a determinative political force for good in the twenty-first century. In responding to this need, the public, private and voluntary sectors, including the Churches and religious communities, must cooperate for the good of all citizens.

Notes

1. Over the fifty years of the existence of the European Communities, the Churches and Christian organisations throughout the Member States have been active players in exploring the human, social–ethical and spiritual significance of the European project in general and of many of its specific policies. They also played an important role in enabling public opinion in the countries of central and eastern Europe to prepare for accession to the EU.
2. The Second Special Assembly of the Synod of Bishops for Europe met in Rome from 1 to 23 October 1999. One of the continental synods in preparation for the millennium, its theme was, 'Jesus Christ, Alive in his Church, the Source of Hope for Europe'.
3. The First Special Assembly of the Synod of Bishops for Europe was convoked by Pope John Paul II in his address at the shrine of Regina Caeli, Velehrad, 22 April 1990. The Synod met from 28 November to 14 December 1991. Its theme was, 'So that We Might be Witnesses of Christ who has set us Free'.
4. For a collection of such provisions, see Robbers (2001).
5. In the Treaty of Amsterdam, Declaration no. 11 on the status of Churches and non-confessional organisations reads as follows:

> The European Union respects and does not prejudice the status under national law of churches and religious associations or communities in the Member States.
> The European Union equally respects the status of philosophical and non-confessional organisations.

These provisions were incorporated into Article 1–52 of the Treaty Establishing a Constitution for Europe.

6. Article 1–52 of the Treaty Establishing a Constitution for Europe states:
    1. The Union respects and does not prejudice the status under national law of churches and religious associations or communities in the Member States.
    2. The Union equally respects the status of philosophical and non-confessional organisations.
    3. Recognising their identity and their specific contribution, the Union shall maintain an open, transparent and regular dialogue with these churches and organisations.

7. A series of EU policy initiatives since 2001 refer to the Churches and religions, whether as contributors to the process of governance, or as players in society who are to be considered in developing policy. Examples are:

   - Commission of the European Communities (2001) *European Governance, A White Paper*, Brussels, 25.7.2001, COM (2001) 428 final;

   - Commission of the European Communities (2005) *The Prevention of and Fight against Terrorist Financing through Enhanced National Level Coordination and Greater Transparency of the Non-profit Sector*, Commission Communication to the Council, The European Parliament and the European Economic and Social Committee, Brussels, 29.11.2005, COM (2005) 620 final;

   - Commission of the European Communities (2005) *A Common Agenda for Integration, Framework for the Integration of Third-Country Nationals in the European Union*, Communication from the Commission to the Council, the European Parliament, the European Economic and Social Committee and the Committee of Regions, Brussels, 1.9.2005, COM (2005) 389 final;

   - Commission of the European Communities (2005), *Terrorist Recruitment: Addressing the Factors Contributing to Violent Radicalisation*, Communication from the Commission to the European Parliament and the Council Concerning, Brussels, 21.9.2005, COM (2005), 313 final.

8. The French original version, *Le Devenir de l'Union Européenne et la Responsabilité des Catholiques*, is available in several translations on the COMECE website (http://www.comece.org/). The document – together with a preface by Cardinal Jean-Marie Lustiger, an introduction by Archbishop Hippolyte Simon, a postscript by Jacques Delors, and other accompanying text – has been published in Commission des Épiscopats de la Communauté Européenne (2006).

9. The Prüm Convention was signed on 27 May 2005 by Belgium, Germany, Spain, France, Luxembourg, the Netherlands and Austria. It covers a wide range of areas of cross-border co-operation: *inter alia*, information exchange, illegal immigration, repatriation, joint-border policing operations, civil crisis management. It requires signature on the part of eight Member States so that it might be brought to the EU as an area of reinforced cooperation. The text of the Convention is available in Council of the European Union (2005)

References

Commission des Épiscopats de la Communauté Européenne (2006) *Les Catholiques et L'Europe*, Paris: Bayard Presse.

Commission of the European Communities (2001) *European Governance: A White Paper*, Brussels, 25.7.2001, COM (2001) 428 final.

Commission of the European Communities (2005) *The Commission's Contribution to the Period of Reflection and Beyond: Plan D for Democracy, Dialogue and Debate*, Communication from the Commission to the Council, the European Parliament, the European Economic and Social Committee and the Committee of the Regions, Brussels, 13.10.2005, COM (2005) 494 final.

Commission of the European Communities (2006) *White Paper on a European Communication Policy*, Brussels, 1.2.2006, COM (2006) 35 final.

Council of the European Union (2005) *Prüm Convention: Note from the Council Secretariat to Delegations*, Brussels, 7 July 2005 (28.07) 10900/05.

Eurobarometer (2005) *Eurobarometer 64: Public Opinion in the European Union* (fieldwork October–November 2005; publication December 2005).

(http://europa.eu.int/comm/public_opinion/archives/eb/eb63/eb63.4_en_first.pdf)

Eurobarometer (2005a) *Eurobarometer 63: Public Opinion in the European Union* (fieldwork May–June 2005; publication July 2005).

(http://europa.eu.int/comm/public_opinion/archives/eb/eb63/eb63.4_en_first.pdf)

Lustiger, Cardinal Jean-Marie (2006) 'L'Europe avant l'Europe', Préface, Commission des Épiscopats de la Communauté Européenne, *Les Catholiques et L'Europe*, Paris: Bayard Presse, pp. 7–14.

Robbers, Gerhard (2001) (ed.) *Religion-Related Norms in European Union Law*. (http://www.uni-trier.de/~ievr/EUreligionlaw/index.html)

von Vietinghoff, Eckhart (2004) 'Heimliche Revolution, Die EU hat ihr Verhältnis zu den Kirchen geklärt – und fast keiner hat es gemerkt', *Zeitzeichen*, 6, 2004, pp. 30–4.